Almond Eyes Hears The Dove's Cries

Almond Eyes Hears The Dove's Cries

Jafar Alam

Foreword by
NAIMA ALAM

Library of Congress Control Number:		2010901663
ISBN:	Hardcover	978-1-4500-3912-3
	Softcover	978-1-4500-3911-6
	Ebook	978-1-4500-3913-0

To order additional copies of this book, contact:
Xlibris Corporation
1-888-795-4274
www.Xlibris.com
Orders@Xlibris.com
75053

Contents

Contents

Contents

Contents

Contents

Contents

Contents

Contents

Contents

Foreword

When my older and indubitably much cooler brother asked me to write the foreword for this book, I didn't realize what an honour it would be. Apparently, not just anyone is asked to write one – only someone who matters. And what in the heck did I do to win this opportunity besides share the same womb, roof, love for poetry and inclination to sappiness? Maybe it was the latter. That's why I'm gonna totally sugar coat all of this to embarrass him. My brother probably doesn't have blood in his veins; he probably has syrup instead. (As in, a lot of sugar in his blood – for those who imagined Maple syrup). I don't think I realized the full extent of his tenderness until I read his poems. Of all people, he has always managed to move me to tears just because of the simple fact that he has always come off as so mysterious to me, and when he divulges so much of himself through his art, it makes me emotional. It's astonishing that he has had such a tough existence, that he has experienced things I've sometimes only learned of through his writing, through his friends, through family, but rarely directly from him. And it was comforting to read about it all in the manuscript and realize that we're so much alike in convictions, goals, desires, experiences, and outlook.

It's reassuring that there are no holds barred. It's also frustrating that he's had to live through so many of the same losses repeatedly. My brother has always given us, his immediate family, the impression that he's a tough guy who's always in control of his feelings. That he doesn't do vulnerable.

Visiting his blog and reading his unpublished work has shown me how naïve I've been to have believed it. Far too many womb mates dread expressing themselves to each other, repulsed by the appearance of weakness, but they don't realize that the more it's hidden, the more it shows, just like any other kind of love. There's still that ridiculous lingering feeling of the need to put up a façade . . . in front of blood. We have been such womb mates. Once upon a time we were children together, but a milestone - his transition from adolescence to adulthood - plunged him into an alternate sphere of mystery that he has never fully recovered from, as is conveyed through his poems, and as is, conversely, diminished through them. It euphemistically makes Bhaiya an enigma. And for so long I've wanted to know what the real Bhaiya is, what kind of mischief he gets himself into, who his friends are, what kinds of thoughts race through his mind, if they're the same as mine, things like that. I get to do that now with this book.

In response to his poem "A Single Tear," let me tell you, he is every parent's sweetest dream. A brother he is and always was. Masha'Allah. He babysat and bathed me in my babyhood, he read bedtime stories to me in adolescence, now in my adulthood, he can sense the punks who talk to me like a hawk eyeing its prey, and he drops me off at my bus terminal, sometimes before sunrise, never complaining no matter how hard it is to keep his eyes open. Even if that means driving through red lights.

"I thought it was green." Haha. Seriously though. And, of course, one of the greatest measures of brotherly love thus far: he allowed me the privilege of publishing this in his book. Look Ma and Abbu! Both your babies are published poets!

Bhaiya, I take pride in knowing you, in the fact that we have exited from the same wound, and in the fact that we have come to share the same art. To know your sadness and humanity, to be welcomed into this warmth, is comforting, because I can relate and it tells me I'm not alone. You've already achieved your purpose with this collection. Thank God for art.One last thing. My poetry might not hold a light to yours, but my gift is my poem, and this one's for you:

I admire your talent and your perception,
Your selflessness, your protection,
Your forbearance, your wisdom.
May your eternity be in Gardens
And God's Mercy your Kingdom.

Something tells me you'll go down in history as the next Langston
Hughes . . . Or one of them Renaissance poets. I just really like the
name Langston Hughes.

Love,
Naima Alam
Your Baby Sister!

Preface

I begin in the name of The Most High

The pages that follow, are a culmination of thoughts, experiences, wishes, hope, advice and wisdom understood throughout my life time. This book does not contain any chapters, nor does it contain any specific theme.

These are merely the voices in my head and the feelings in my heart expressed on paper.

Therefore, we can say that you are about to enter into my mind.

I wish to share this gift with others, in the hopes that those who can relate, may understand that they are not alone.

I do not claim any rank nor seek any sort of position. My reward is with my Lord.

Enough words . . . Here is a part of my soul . . . A part of me . . . Some pages of my poetry.

Welcome to my world

Peace and Blessings,

Jafar S B Alam

Dedications

I begin in the name of God, for giving me life and all that comes with it . . . I ask Him to help and heal me . . .

This book is dedicated to my mother, my father and my sister . . . You leave me wordless. I love you a love I can never put into words.

To Maryam Noori (Almond eyes), you are a blessing from the Most High. I will forever be indebted to you . . .
Thank you for your care, your concern, for keeping me in check, the wisdom and the life time of memories. Thank you for the gift of poetry. Thank you for introducing me to Ahmed. Thank you, for being such an honorable friend.

To Ahmed Hussain, you sparked something inside of me that's never been touched. I love you and miss you dearly my friend.
I dedicate this book to you and I thank your mother and father for bringing something so beautiful into this world.
God Willing, we will be with the ones that we love. Rest In Peace.

This book is dedicated to Dolly (QT), for believing in me and seeing in me, what I never saw in myself. I will always pray for you the salaam of Heaven and Earth.

To Shoaib Khan, thank you for everything you've ever done for me bro, and encouraging me to share my poetry with the world.

This book is dedicated to my beautiful grandparents, my aunts, uncles, cousins, neices and nephews . . .

This book is dedicated to Hamza Yusuf, for showing a little boy light, after he was in darkness.

Dedications

To my aunt Nabila, thank you for being a mother and a friend and for all the waffle dates . . . Love u . . .

To Wafa, my spokenword sidekick . . . Tea and poetry . . . Respect for all the convo sessions and intellectual quotes . . . Empress . . .

To Jameela Jaber, thank you so much for giving me the opportunity to share my poetry on your stage . . . Ya'nee . . .

To Tristan Raghunan, a beautiful sound makes the world go round . . . You are amazingly talented my friend . . .

To Sabiha Iqbal, for all the help on this book and all the support and laughs . . .

This book is dedicted to the pen and the paper . . . To poetry . . . To the stage . . . To the microphone . . .

To the Capri 5
To my teachers
To the martial arts
This book is dedicated to the lovers
The dreamers
The liars
The hypocrites
This book is dedicated to childhood
To innocence
To memories
To my heart
To my unborn child
To poverty
To hope

To laughter
This book is dedicated to the lost and found
This book is dedicated to those who prayed for this book
This book is dedicated to the heartbreakers
To Hip Hop
To the 80's and the 90's
To sleepless nights and heavy hearts
To Rumi
To solitude
This book is dedicated to LOVE and SORROW
To tears
To the sun
To the rain
To fear
To the train and the discman
This book is dedicated to silence
To my car "Mudhu", for all the long drives
This book is dedicated to time
To intellect
To creativity
To passion
This book is dedicated to art, culture and life
To sweet tea and prayer beads
To all those, who I've had the good fortune of knowing
This book is dedicated to the past, present and future . . .

Letter to Maryam

I have chosen to title this work "Almond Eyes Hears The Dove's Cries" in the hopes of honouring you, a friend, who showed me the light of poetry. In this short lifetime, that at times feels like an eternity, I have come across so many unique indivuals. Each person brought their own lasting impression. However, none have been able to do, what you almond eyes, have been able to do. If angels are created from light,then you Maryam, are light upon Earth. There is pain in your voice, praise on your tongue, love in your heart and depth in your soul. That in itself, makes you beautiful.

In a lot of traditional spiritual poetry, the "dove", is symbolic of the soul.

I wanted to honour you, for everything you've done for me, despite all the things you've gone through. I know your soul still cries, but He (The Most High) will comfort those tears for you soon, as we both await to answer the call of the Caller when He calls.

My teacher once told me:
"There is light at the end of the tunnel, for those who want light"

I have no doubt that there is something beautiful waiting for you, for everything that you've patiently endured in your life my friend.

My wish, is to be there on the day that you receive it. You have been a pillar of strength and a beacon of light for so many.

An inspiration, for those who have had the good pleasure of knowing you. Though you may feel that you are nothing in this world, you Maryam Noori, were here.

Simply put, you are the greatest friend that I have ever had. I thank you, for all that you are.

All praises are for God. He does nothing less than perfect.

So, may He steal from you, ALL, that steals you from Him.

I pray that both you and Ahmed are given gardens, from the Gardens of Paradise. Ameen.

Love,
Peace,
Blessings,
and Saffron tea . . .

Jafar

"*. . . but my soul is just a whisper trapped inside a tornado . . .*"
- Kimya Dawson

Almond Eyes Hears The Dove's Cries

Love Hurts *(For all of my nieces)*

Love hurts

Even when we act like
We're bulletproof

And yet

Love is how
We get through it

You are a gem

If any guy tells you
"You're worthless"

Don't give him no
Eargasm

Punch that fool in the face

Tell em
"Fool, you just got dissed and dismissed"

And then

Skip away

The Best Kept Secret

Now

I'm not one to say
Never

But
Never again
Would I want to see you hurt

Let the wind
Chill your rage

And a fire
Mix with sage

Free a spirit from your eyelid
And let it hug the night sky

You make me feel
Some sorta way

You are the best kept secret

You are magic

Why don't you
Help raise the future

With your lessons
Of experience

Motivate your smile
Maryam

Through my pain and hurt
People tell me they find
Beautiful poetry

I smile

I'll take that compliment
Off of them

Cause I know
It's from the heart

Honour the ocean of
Love

You look good

You look like you're your own
Daughter

Your life is a gorgeous puzzle
Learn to appreciate all the pieces

If anyone asks you
"Where's your Lord?"

Tell them
"He is near"

People will eventually learn the language

Of God

Take Her By The Hand

There is a place
Where you are not alone

You make my love
Come down

There's an amazingly beautiful
Poetic
Old Soul type
Essence to you

Giiiirl

Your dreams
Are not negotiable

Your feelings of love
Are only a guide
For what you'll give for love

You are a promising gift
Of light and soul

Hope is waiting for you
To take her by the hand

Tiptoe into your dreams

There is a fire burning somewhere
Waiting to warm you

Don't give up
On your future

In The Arms Of Midnight

Chocolate girl

Your hair looks
Un-beweaveable

Don't give up on tomorrow
It's already praisin'
Today

You aint a regular
Earth dweller

Sweet heart
There's only one caste system . . .
That's the human race

And Karma

She's a trip

She's got their names
In her book

You deserve a love
That makes you a priority
Not an option hun

Don't run away from your problems
Lest you start avoiding mirrors

Chocolate girl

You're the realist fairytale

Don't try explaining yourself
To them

How you explain sunshine
To a blind man?

You are the joy of the world

Yeeeeup!

So act like it

Gwan!
Gwan!

Don't be some fools
Baby mama

Boilin' milk over a stove
With lost dreams

These boys
These days

They be fallin' in love
Without love

Don't be so consumed
With the world around you
That you neglect the world
Within you

Start your journey

If they ask for you

Tell em

They can find you
Waiting in the dimple of a moon
In the arms of midnight

Dancing
To the whistle

Of the wind

Another Story

You got your own swag and charm

And yet
You still bathe
In tears

Have a long
Introspective conversation
With yourself

Love is as real
As the One
Who created it

Now
You're losin' hope
In humanity?

Child,

That's another story
For
Another day

Chocolate Boy

Chocolate boy
Is a beautiful
Soul

Soul journeying
For
Soul food

If you count him out
Then you
Miscounted

Jafar Alam

Timing Is Divine *(For Ahmed and Maryam)*

I stare at the frozen smile
Of my long deceased
Friend

At that moment

Maryam calls
And says:

Love is real

Dear Grandma *(For my late grandmother . . .*
Rest In Peace)

No man is equal
To a woman

You were
Nine times
Baby swollen

And a tale
To be told

There was a humming felt
In our gaze

Remembering our
Existential type
Conversations

Your voice echoes
Through my
Place of person

Your influence
Was fluid

Words may fail me
When it comes to you

Wrestling against
The pull and tear
Of the wind

You
Are missed

The Slave And The Master

The slave asked
The master
To find him a wife

The master told
The slave
To find himself first

Unveiled Moon *(Dedicated to a little girl named Safa)*

In a sky filled
With studded stars

An
Unveiled moon
Appears

How flawless
Is your beauty

That Night

On that night
My heart
Tore apart

I cried
In my best friends arms

Till I couldn't cry
Anymore

Tired

I left

And took myself
To sleep

A New Day

You are receding
From my mind

There is a darkness
That we share

As I sit
Under a naked
Light bulb

Your hollow voice
Fades

A new day
Arrives

Good morning
Life

Let My Words Die

Your raspy voice
Still lingers
In my ear

I looked past
The head wrap
And tried to wrap my head
Around this . . .

What did I ever do
To be given a gift
Like you?

Tomorrow
The Angel of Death
Will come for me

So today
Let my words die

In your heart

Purple Sky

I thought
I was fly

Cool
Like a Fall night

Street dreams

Now I'm just tryina live
Un-apologetically

Love is sacrifice

Tryina help others
Through my own suffering

Through
Life's wisdom

I stopped
To park my car aside
For a conversation
With the wind

Not sure
What my heart would say
To my body
If it could write a letter

The world right now
Is breathtakingly beautiful

You're a special kind
Of magic

Almond eyes
The sun shines
On your face
As the shadows
Of leaves
Reflect
Through your window

You made my emotions
Make sense

Ignorance
Is also a part
Of me

I prayed for you

Never stopped praying

A good friend
Is good medicine

Smile through pain
Maryam

Life will teach you
That there are reasons
To smile
Everywhere

And right now
I'm in love

With this
Purple sky

Summer Rain

The sound
Of water

The sound
Of earth

Everywhere

A summer rain

In My Nephews Eyes

Love
Makes its way
Around the heart

When
Praise is continual
On the tongue

And the soul
Is penetrated

In my nephews eyes
I see
Eternity

Fake Poets

Their moment in the sun
Will soon come to pass

Fake
Undercover
Wannabe
Poets

Content with the recycled garbage
They produce

How much praise
Do you need
Before you've had
Your fix?

It aint talent
To re-word
Re-produce
Previous works

You're not a poet
You're a plagiarist

If you have nothing to say
Don't say it

You got dreams
Then dream your own reality

Why don't you
Commit yourself
To something other than
Yourself

You aint givin' a voice
To the
Voiceless streets

You aint an eye
Among the
Blind

You're real . . .

Fake

She Told Me

Almond Eyes told me
I should train my mind
So that I'm not embarassed by my thoughts

Reminded me that
God looks into our hearts
And reads it

She told me
To speak to people
On their level

The path is hard

Many days
We agree on
Disagreeing

Her words always find shelter
In my heart

Maryam
You are a deeply rooted hand
In the soil
Of our bettering

And poetry
Is how we arrange the world
Around us

The Travel Of Your Gaze

Your face, pure light
Remains a flickering candle
In the lonely dark

The waters of my soul
Stir

Long days
And
Short nights

Blood still beats
In our hearts

The night becomes enlarged
By sounds

The rain has begun
Shaking its hair out
Onto the streets

I sit in my car
Thinking of you

Trying to numb the pain
Of existence

Summers
Repeated and ended
In heartbreak

Your scent
Too rich for keeping
Too light to remember

I was born to lie
You were born to listen

In these rented minutes of life
Your name's still on my tongue

I want to sing again
With the tones of youth

Our chests
Like the Grand Canyon
Spread empty over the world

We are perfectly
Lovely

I want to see the world that exists
Behind the beauty of your eyes

The trees
Are black against the sky
At dusk
The last dove cries

I want to be
The travel
Of your gaze

Under The Sultans Tent

Under the sultans tent
A young girl dances
With her belly

Eight men stare
Six forget they are married

Like camel nomads

Her hair
Like the setting sun
Her eyes
A sparkling star

There is a breaking sadness
In her voice

Something of this shackled slave
Sobs in the rhythm
Of the music

She was born
For sorrows mate

I can visualize her alone

A girl
Harbouring her cryptic thoughts

A small
Insignificant person
That won't be remembered
By the rest of the world

Young Algerian girl sends me a message:
"May you be given a wife, like the moon.
She'll disappear by day, and appear by night."

Under the sultans tent
A young girl dances
With her belly

Eight men stare
Six forget they are married

They utter filth
I refuse to repeat

Those who know
Are more accountable

Than those
Who know not

Wanting Love

I don't wanna ruin love
By wanting it so bad

But I kinda want love
So that my heart
Comes out of its hiding place

Sweet dreaming

Hopeless outlook

We do not know
The strength
Of our own
Power

Calm The Fire

The words did not reach
My soul

Clouds and mist
Cover the sky

The dance see's
No age (the dance with the devil)

Calm the fire
In your soul

Almond eyes
I imagine us reclining in a garden
In some beautiful land
Under a tree of cherry blossoms

As we pray to Allah
To protect us
From the darkness
Inside our souls

Everything starts to fade
In a veil of tears

As the tears
Cleanse our hearts

The fear of my sins
Grabbing hold of my soul

And dragging it
Into the bowels of Hell

Are playing
In my head

Fana

The sky came to me
Smiling

Truth
Finally sank
Into my soul

My mother prayed
Against what the world
Would make hard for me (love)

Emotional violence

So many friends disappeared
Into the Earth

An aura of Jasmine
Follows me

There's nothing I could say
That you don't already know
In your heart

I looked into the face
Of Death

Dead bodies are carpeting
The Earth

If there's purpose

Where's the meaning?

Everyone has
Their own camps
Their own shops

The doors of this heart
Are always Open

There's no closed shop here

My hands are free
My help is free

The purpose of knowledge
Is to inspire us
Divinely

Come out of
Ana

To enter
Fana

Their Dreams *(Dedicated to my mother and father)*

A couple embrace
Each other
Under a shelter
In the rain

He whispers a sweet something
Into her smile

Maybe one day
Their dreams
Will come true

The Ocean Of Time

There is a forced reflection
That comes
With every loss

Like a first love
Always remembered
Gladly
In the past

A passing wave
in the ocean
Of time

What You Need

What you need
Is in need of
Today

What is this tomorrow
You speak of ?

Mirrors Of Your Eyelids

Fog
On the mirrors
Of your eyelids

Tear stained cheeks

Humming prayers
Between clenched fists
Holding prayer beads

You carried your heart
On your sleeve

And bled
Through the seems

Now
You imagine windows

To a new lovers heart

For Ahmeds Mom *(Mubasher Hussain)*

Under a freckled Spring sky

Your breath
Grazed his cheek

As his laughter
Disturbed the wind

You are
A steady storm
A field of shivering flowers

A rusted goodbye
Lays gently against your ear

You are miracle

Forever *(To Almond Eyes)*

As your last words sink
Into my heart

The Angel of Death
Leans down
In terrifying proximity

You
Kept me wrapped
In love

Your cries
Tearing the hole in my heart
Wider

At that moment
I fell in love with you
All over again

After an eternity
That was only
A moment

We were still connected
At the heart

We had chosen
Forever

A last breath let out
From our hearts

Like a freed dove
Flying away
To Heaven

Lets Walk, Ahmed

You have tasted the death
That your Lord
Had sent for you

There are
No more deaths
After this

If we are to meet
At the bridge

Lets walk
Hand in hand

To eternity

Loves Rain

Misty eyes
Scan the sky

An empty vessel
Sings praises
Of His name

Waiting for light
To eradicate
Darkness

Loves rain
Pours on the earth
And showers the hearts

Only the ones cut by it
Understand the agony
Of the knife

In Your Prayers

Waiting for angels
To take us to
Heaven or
Hells abode

To dwell within forever

Those words
Put out the last fire
Of worldy love
In my heart

Faith was embraced that night
And a kiss
From the wind

You asked me how I wanted to be remembered
After I have passed

I can only ask
That you
Remember me

In your prayers

Veiled Souls

Veiled souls

Let us meet
In the timelessness of
Love

Enlightened people
Have never been understood
By the majority

Many say
They seek Truth

When
In reality
They want to believe
The things they love
As Truth

Ignorance
Is a veil

Hiding
The Truth

From our eyes

To My Unborn Child

My child
I imagine your words
Stirring in my heart

With a soft voice
And a tongue of honey

Innocence flowing
Like silk in a breeze

Your heart
As soft as a dove

A wind blows by
And in it
I hear your laughter

One day
You will jump
From my hands
Into my heart

Causing my heart
To swell with love

And I will try my best

To teach you
The ancient ways
Of this worldly life

I want your soul to fly
To a world of dreams
And laughter
Through possibilities
And adventure

Your smile
Will speak to me

The years will become minutes
Until I will forget
Time

I will pour my soul
To you

As your laughter
Caresses my heart

You will give me
A new birthday

I
Your daddy
With all my flaws
Will try to teach you
As I continue to discover
Myself

I wanna to tell you about
God

I wanna teach you
Not to obey any created thing
If it means
Disobedience to the
Creator of things

Trying to master
The art of
Patience

Sweet child
You are a light
Of hope
Lit in my heart

I'm waiting for you
That together
We can both await
The coming of the
Holy Messiah

I pray that
He delivers you
To this world

Before

He delivers me
From this world

Child
There is a valuable lesson
In learning
To let go

Smiling
Is a form of prayer
Pray

Feel me on this
The louder you scream
The less they'll listen

Develope relationships

Search for beauty

Beauty in the breakup
And in the
Breakdown

My child
The sun will smile
When it see's you

Ask me
Of Love
I will tell you
Love can be defined
As the
Undefinable

And I wait for the day
That you will tell me stories
With your fathers
Imagination

Paint me a picture
And take me there

I am a dreamer
You
The dream
I don't want to wake up

Kid
You're the vocal chords
To some heaven
I imagine in my head

Maybe you will
One day
Inherit your mothers
Curiosity

I serve Him
By honoring
Her

My child
People rarely respect beauty
So be more than just
A pretty
Or
Handsome face

I'll teach you to
Love yourself
You'll see
It works wonders

I can't wait
To share
Sunshine and apple juice

You
Telling
Me
I'm out of shape
Like a cookie
With a bite in it

Me
Seeing in you
What you might not
See in yourself

I hope you never
Love
To
Hate

Hope you're as
Inquisitive
As your aunt

With the youthful spirit
Of your grandmother

The ambition
Of your grandfather

I pray
That you are one of the
Forces of light
The world has been pushing for

I look forward
To the inspiring hope
You bring

To this world

I remind myself
Before I remind you to
Remain present
And responsible
To your voice
And stories

The thoughts of you
Are humbling

Remember that
Everyone has an incredible
Spiritual and emotional truth to them
Use it
To keep you in check
On life's journey

I wish I could just
Find your smile

Wish I could
Hug you

Your mom and I wait
To kiss you
And kiss you
Until the origin of the kiss
Explains itself

And these chocolate fingers
Will throw you up and catch you
Sugar
We wait to hear the heartfelt laughter

From you

I will fight with swords
Against Love and Reason
Just to cause sparks that will compete to be
The light in your eyes
When you wake to me

My child
I ask nothing from you
Just your presence
When your are present

I await your arrival

There is a room
In my heart
Still empty

Hurry

Love,
Dad

Till The End Of Time

He walks down
An empty street
His head lowered in awe
Of the grandeur
Of his Lord

A Creator
Closer to us
Than our own
Reality

A prayer
Cannot be read
It must be felt

The ground
Was cold and moist
Feeling as if
He had been sealed
Within a grave

Satanic messages
And
Distorted sounds
Could be heard

The breath of the
Final hour
Is cold

Screams
Sounding like a thousand bolts
Of lightning

The fear of death
Creeps upon them

Their cries
Of terror
Quickly silenced

History's been
Manipulated
To keep you in
The dark

The sky wept
For what it had seen

The shadow of death
Hangs above

The screaming winds
Echoe

A blanket of silence
Follows

Truth remains Truth
Till the end
Of time

Q

My love
Lay buried deep
In the void of my heart

The hidden well
Of emotion
Was released

My words
Settled gently
On your soul that night

I lived
A thousand lifetimes

Everything stopped
As if time
Held its breath

The wind rose
And began to sing

I felt your beauty
Radiating
From inside this dreamworld

That you alone
Seem to occupy

I haven't seen anything

So lovely

It is through your eyes
That I feel
Special

Marose

Butterfly winged petals
Scattered in the wind

Hair knots
Untangled

The rebirth of
Our souls

Lost souls
And
Perfect strangers

Our loss
Was Heavens gain

Breathing the sorrow
Into your soul

You were
My difference

You came
And left
Like a winded breath

We first met
With eyes
Then
Honeyed words

The wind rose

Faiths paradox

A battle
Between the soul
And the flesh

My inner me
Is my enemy

And
You and I
Parted

Like
The Red Sea

The Humble Hustle

I wanna love
Until there is no need to understand
And just be

Like profound wonder

I wanna read poems that dance
Beautifully
On the ear

Everyday's
Another chance

The humble hustle
Continues

Appreciating the listener
In you

I've never really told anyone
This stuff before

I guess
I'm a glutton for
Love

Ok
That's all
Peace out

Flames Of Eternity

They observed
The cover of darkness

The horizon was covered
In mist

The scent of death
Was lurking above

Sometimes shattering
Soft hearts

His soul already matured
Past many life times

The last flame of ego
Was put out

Fear
Veiled her heart

Illusions vanishing
Into the night air

Chains of hope
Were wrapped
Around their hearts

The flames of eternity
Were ignited

Adrian *(Dedicated to my childhood friend Adrian Bannerman, who was killed in July, 2008)*

The words reach the heart
Of my ear

A lost boy
Convinced of manhood

I am weak to the touch
Of the Earth

Clumsy for attention

Confused
In my souls expression

Each day
Is a new prayer

Bullets clip off
In Eastmall

The beauty of your voice
Comes through
From between your lips

And to die
Is in itself
An adventure

Dealing Out Love

Dealing out love
Like springs of water
Bursting open
And showering out

His heart
Flew into his throat

Ahmed, my brother
On that day
The sky darkened

And your heart
Forgot to beat

I wish I had the chance
To live the good
Of your company

Just once

And a prayer was prayed
That you be in a garden
From the Gardens of Paradise

Almond eyes
We were the two wings
Of a dove
Flying in beauty

Images of you
Sowed in a field of love

Now I'm falling
Into a bottomless pit
Of darkness

The bitter sweet beauty
Of love

In The Still Night

A quiet soul

The journey of my life
Bringing me to this moment

Your words
Branded on my heart

Our gazes met

Heart wrenching cries
Echoed

You hold a place in my heart
That no one could ever touch

I felt a chill
In the still humid night

As I entered a dream

Peace In Paradise

Since you came
My heart has smiled

Since you left
My lips cannot

Ancient breezes
Still blowing

My cries
Were greeted with silence

There will be peace
In Paradise

You were just
A piece of Heaven

Given
To me

Bound To Happen

The moon has taken its leave
And the world remains lit
Only by the stars

A silence falls
Like the stillness of night
Before the birth of dawn

My face betrayed anger

If I had one wish
If I could close my eyes
And open it
I would want you to ask me
A thousand and one questions again

Your secrets
Are in my trust

You are the bridge
Between me and my sanity

Bruises heal

I was bound to happen
You were bound to happen

Hush that mouth

The audience is internal

With reserved seating

Don't let them distract you

Thinking Of Ahmed

The clouds
Hugged the sky

By the Will
Of the Most Generous

Giving his last breaths
Ahmed went
To live
In my heart

Remembering
The crescent smile
On your face

Your wind blown cheeks
Red and round

Questions
Left
Unanswered

Sleep avoids
My longing
Soul

Poetic Floetry

The material
And the spiritual world
Meet at every corner
Until the time arrives to give birth to
Poetry

And the poetic flowetry flows
As the poets flow
Gives birth to a new poem
For every seed that it sows

Intoxicating each one with the soma
Of a dead poets prose

Each word
Breathing life
Into the empty crevices
Of lost souls

Uprising

Verbal intercourse
What the poets crave

Offering freedom
Like an emancipated

Berber slave

And mother Earth
Gave birth
To poetry

Holding poets
In their infancy

Singing
"Hush little baby, don't you cry
For I'd feed you the truth
Before I ever fed you a lie"

And the words of the righteous
Live on
Even after
They die

In The Coma Of The Night

In the coma of the night

Thoughts of you
Spread like petals in the wind

Inside this sauna summer

Too afraid
To swallow your heart again

You
Soft organic

Tip toed
Into my life

Praise

Suffer like a martyr

We've all been called
Only a few
Will respond

The last to die
Is
Hope

Lyrical vibrations
Of praise
Engulf the whole
Of the Earth

Send your love
To the well wishers

Standing
By the heart

You are a sun
Risen

We took a covenant
Before life
In the womb

O my love
Pray

As the breezes of your breath
Blow

And in the silence
A pulse
Beats

Live

As we bug out

Don't go
Trying to save the world

Until
You confront the world
That lies within you

Consider the complexities
Of your own heart
Before you go makin'
An attempt at others

Continue to flourish
In the beauty
Of all
That is you

Life aint long

If ever
There was a time
To live

It's now
Or never

In this body
Of a soul

Within these
Perfumed walls

LIVE

The World Is A Dream

Happiness is dancing
On your tongue

Robbed of cloud nine

I may not understand
The language of your tongue

But I understand
The language
Of your eyes

The signs of love
Are on every lover

Photo's
Are just memories

Scrap that

There is no
Depression

Just my anger
Turned inwards

The deeper the love
The deeper the loss

This world

Is a dream
Often mistaken
For reality

Darkness
Entombs us

The eye
Satiated itself
Thinking it filled
What the heart
Was craving

I didn't know
What I needed
Until I lost
What I had

I wanna subdue the enemy
Without harming them

And conquer the battle
Before the war

In This Moment

The veil
Of night
Hides behinde
The light of day

They
Lived their lives
Outside of time
Living only
In the moment
Given to them

The scent of those moments
Embedded
In their hearts

The two were blessed
And cursed
With perfect memory

A vivid imagination

Disproportionately
Nostalgic

A sudden concern
About a future
Yet
To come

Their worries
Splintering them
Forever

All that matters
All that lives
Is now
In this moment of
Eternity

Conversation With Myself

Cot Damn !!

I just keep on
Keepin' on

Life is full of its own
Kinda splendor

I'm a well
Of lost and found
Things

Blessed
To still be here

To tell the story of
My overcoming

Enjoying the breath
That's been entrusted
To me

And
Learning to be
More comfortable

In my own honesty

O Prophet

Prostrated on the earth

Your enemy
Draws nearer

All that you need
Sits within you

What remains outside of you
Is but
Your own desires

You were not sent
To send
To Hell

O Prophet
Remain firm

They will gather their people
To harm you

Know that your Lord
Will send
The angels of Hell

To defend you

Jafar Alam

Flowers From Babylon

The rain buffeted
Throughout the city

I went to buy flowers
From Babylon

You smiled at me
Apologetically

A silence
Fell over me

So deep
I could hear the cries
Of the soul

Looking at you
Through reborn eyes
Darkness takes over me
Yet again

A darkness
So deep

That all thoughts leave
And only silence

Remains

Song Of One Breath

Loneliness
Bleeding
Into my life

Knees lookin' like they've been
Prayin' in flour

She walks in beauty
Like the night

The lingo of the pen
No longer ancient

I am not afraid
Of the world

No shadows float
Across the window pane

The image blurs

In this night
The moon breaks through the clouds

There is a single smile
Which I touch

From which
In my thirst
I drink

Roasted
By your passion

I love you
With all my heart

Why don't you love me
With yours

I'll love you
Forever and ever

The song
Of one breath

Wordless

The wind
Breaths loudly

I was thinking
Of you

Godless people
Live in a
Godless world

I wanted to
Come to your
Rescue
To arrest you
Rest you
And your mind
Your head on my shoulder

They say
If you come on heavy
You will lose
Your people

I held your attention
And touched
Your soul

Emotions flow
Through my writing

There's no sameness
In beauty

Unceasing devotion
To the breath
And the name of
God

Grab me
Before I fly by

Find me a seat
To be closer
To Him

Birth this poet
With your energy

I love you
A love
I can't describe

Dance in my heart

Tomorrow
Isn't promised
To us

Trying to describe you
The words are endless

And I
Am left

Wordless

Prayer On My Lips

We are the product of
Two
From
One Source

The smell of wet earth rises

Slow summer days
Of love

We smiled into the dark night

Our voices
Sewing together new life
With the broken pieces
Of our relationships

My eyes smiling at you

The laughter in your eyes
Making love return
To steal my heart

This day
Cloaked in the mist

I missed you
You were a prayer
On my lips

Time melts away

We look at each other
Like it was our
First love

The wind sends its cold fingers
Through the window

I wanted to touch the pulse
At your throat

Love was lost
My love

Like a gentle breeze

Its return
Was sweet

I want you to see
What I see

I see beauty
So long
As my gaze
Is upon you

Nostalgic Poet

A new day takes its first breath
As morning wakes
And dew drops form
On a flowers lips
And clouds gently dance in the winds

I love me some you

I love that reassuring smile
When you catch me out of line

That smile
Containing within it
All that is between Heaven and Earth

The sun's light reaches through a crack in the window
A soft light rests on the tip of your brow lines

The smoke curling upwards from the ashtray
An old man is spending money on this suffering

At some point
We are all guilty of materialism

The old man says

"Closets are for clothes.
You can't avoid temptation
But you don't have to give in"

And people will use religion to manipulate you
They will use it as an excuse to justify their
Political beliefs

Many have a false perception of beauty
And anorexic ideals

I didn't choose poetry
Poetry chose me
So that I could be left alone
To speak to people

Material things
Do not define me

A nostalgic poet

I want to take ignorance
And
Bury it

I want to celebrate you

I don't think
I feel

You are the poem of my memory
The music to my dreams

In the bowels of Hell
Are those
Who brought their own fire

The more you get
The more you want

It's
An addiction

My deceased brother said
"The hell with the first amendment
My speech was free
Even as my soul descended"

We are seekers
We are wanderers

We are
Looking for
Hoping for
Wishing for
Begging for

God

I Wanna

The poet in me
Wants to wait a million moons and suns
For you

I wanna break through that barrier
Around your heart

How can I deny
Full conversations
With just our eyes?

Don't ever close
Your lovely eyes
A pool of clear glass
In which I drown

I wanna dash you in the rain
And serinade you with love poems
And kidnap you in my dreams

I wanna tell my momma
All about you

Like summer rain

I wanna have my sleep stolen
By thoughts of you

I wanna make you
My tomorrow

I wanna call you on restless days
And sleepless nights

I wanna know
If your heart
Skipped a beat

You are light
You are a mystery

And so

A shadow danced for every candle that was lit
And a lie was given birth to
For every secret that was held

Mirror's Don't Lie

Smiles disguise
Their vile thoughts

Mirror's
Don't lie

Drained souls

They've accepted
Death

Without understanding
Life

Always In Love

We had made our covenant with silence

The storm dances with doves

This morning I woke up to love

To be able to see your face
Is itself
Proof of the existence
Of beauty

As perfume gives a scent by itself
It needs not the seller
To describe it

How can your beauty be compressed
Into the structure of words?

I wanna make you secure
Of all your insecurities

I am in love
With love

If there is no love
Then all these laws and religions
Become nothing but idols
Of whimsical ideas

Many have become arrested

By a love
For the materials of this world

We thought the earth and the sky to be boundless
Until we fell in love
And completed the journey

You were worried
That I would become bored

I told you that the ones who get bored
Are the ones who have done too much
And so
They want variety

You wanted to be happy

I was crossing my heart
Hoping to die

At that moment
You became upset

I appologized

I will live with you forever

Many lovers
Lie buried under the earth

The heart is always in love
With someone

It is never a loss
It is a lesson

This Prayer

The third eye see's
What the first two don't

There are those who use
The sacred texts
To turn people into slaves

The moonwalker said
"Fame and fortune, they're all illusions"

Is there room
For that hopeless sinner?

I'm a Muslim
But my message is universal

I was washing my faith
In filthy water

His Beauty
Increases in my eyes
The longer I look in awe

And Ahmed left
But he still lives in this heart

And because he lives on
After his passing
We are thankful to God
That he did not die

Rather
He reached his Friend

And so

I swear
By my friends lost soul

I pray for those
Who have come
And those
Who have left
And those
Who are on their way

That the lovers
Be together again
In that moment of eternity

And I pray
That He
Showers His Mercy
Upon the one who says
"Ameen"
For this prayer

Hello

There's a beautiful energy in the air

May this sparkle of a day
Shine bright

You don't have to do everything
But you could do something

Don't get "high" and relax into stupidity

Time
She passes away from the world

Blooming in the depth

Loving you was easy
At one time

There is a laughter and song
Outside my window

On my way home
To be rescued by the comfort

Upon meeting the sky
I flew

Bathing in this soul

Night love tearing the sky
Into open arms

I'm a man
With the imagination of a child

I wanna breath love
Like air
It's suffocating otherwise

Your heart is a shore I wash up on
After the storm

Walking home in the silence of T.O's chest
In awe of the way the air settles
After the rain

Love and hate are two ships
Passing in the night

Prayer is my antidote for restlessness

Rain showers

You are asleep

While the world
Hums you into lullaby

I'm thinking of you
And how beautifully
You wear sunshine

And as much as I want to be left alone
I can't stand the silence

Thunder and lightning are knocking on my window
I guess the rain has to
Speak its piece

Hello yesterday
Remember how it used to be?

Looks like it's going to be a beautiful day
I'm breathing

Life goes on within you
And
Without you

There are dreams that cannot be
And
Storms you cannot weather

Some people are so disgusting
With disrespect

"Ouch" said my heart
To my chest

The sun appears in the sky
Proud and smiling

Dear Sunday
I like surprises

What a beautiful noise
This city makes

I love the sound of rain
In the city

Telling myself the day is going great
Inspite of what isn't

I'm tryina focus on

What is

New ideas
Don't sound familiar

I think I wanna die
Toothless and madly in love

Hello Sunday
Make me smile

The breeze is a lovely friend

When the wind touches you
The way it sometimes touches me
Smile

I'm sore
My body's yelling at me

Tryina catch my dreams
Before they catch me

Dear Monday
I love the way the sun looks on you

Cut Deeper

Taste my tears

Like a rose
She was silky
But full of thorns

If tomorrow comes
I'll be waiting for life
To punish me
For all my wrong doings

A thing of beauty
The soul will never die

Cut deeper
The poet needs to bleed
In order to tell you his story

The Sun Kissed Your Eyes

We are done with tears

The air is gentle and lay pressed
Against my shoulder like a sleepy child

The sun kissed your eyes

You are a pocket full of lillies
Laughing in the soil of my hand

I'm thinking about the future
In the present

Hips striding
Souls giggling

New beginnings
Are hibernating in our hearts

Spring has sprung

Laughter is truly contagious

Your smile grows in my eyes
Like a last breath

The moon is a chewed finger nail
In the sky

We sit together
Enjoying the rhythm of wind on skin

There is a poem
At the brink of breaking in your eyes

We look at each other
Smiling
In shyness

I want to plant a garden of memory
On your skin

Laughter spreads its wings
In your dimple
And I
Want to take a nap in the nape
Of your neck

Captivated by the moments of today
Reflection is a beautiful thing

I want this moment to splinter
Into joy and wonder
For you
I
Want to be what's needed
What's necessary

Your eyes are bottomless

I'm glad the sun remembers this sky

Dancing with smiles in this warm breeze
Darlin'
Hopefully we'll catch each other

In the silence
The self is echoing

Asking to be listened to

I love when you call
Right at the moment I'm thinking of you

Writing my restlessness away

Turning nerves into passion
And surrendering to the moment

I don't mind the way the rain sifts through your hair
But just remember to smile

Days like this
Are truly worth living for

Laughter is great medicine

I wanna squeeze the sun to jelly
And smear its sparkle all over you

I stayed up till the wee hours of the morning
Talking to you

I wrote you a poem
You called me romantic

My father was a romantic
It's in my blood

I hope to visit you soon

We'll see
Where the wind takes me

Fugazi

You are who you are
And do what you do

To my ears
Your rap
Is a wrap

You are dead for I
I
Am dead for you

You have flavours of the month

You dream in different languages

Bottle that
Don't sell it

Diamonds deserve diamonds

You . . .

You're a fugazi

Mr. Safi

Mr. Safi said that
We're fighting
For reasons other than
What God revealed

And colour is only skin deep

If we really understood humanity
We'd fight for each other

I said

"Sir, I have a problem"

He said

"We are the answer to our problems.
People don't want to change themselves
But they want to change the results"

I remained silent

Symbols In Moments

The rains of love and death
Are showering you and I

There is no way to unlove
This memory of us

I haven't seen your mother in a while
I miss her in your smile

There is a bend in my soul

These poems I write
Can never articulate what I feel

They are just symbols in moments

With each cry
Something dies within me

My heart is heavy

A starving insomniac
I want sanity
But my heart is black

I hope your heart gets torn out one day
And thrown aside

I will come and pick it up

I will hold it in my hand

And squeeze

And at that moment

You too

Will feel the pain
That you put me through

Perhaps

I
Was born in the Fall [love] of '82

You
Don't know what you want
But you know how to get it

Bathing in a love built on dreams
You were surged in my heart

We are together only for as long
As this day will last

In the twilight hour
We will return back

Perhaps to meet again

Soon

Hidden Gem

They always said
What they never meant

The little boy listened

And because they
Couldn't control their words
They weren't able to teach
And he wasn't able to learn

So he thought

Until he started extracting
Meaning
From everything

Then realizing

That the more we learn
The less mistakes we're
Supposed to let ourselves make

The Wali

He is a
Wali of Allah
He gives life to the night
With prostrations

His daughter tells him:

"Baba, you don't stay with us long enough
When you come to visit"

He says:

"I know my child"

She says:

"When you're far away,
I feel like sitting with my father.

But when you're with me,
I feel like I'm sitting with Allah"

Friends Of God

Those who love God
Are the intimates of God

Only the lovers
Can recognize the lovers

Those who do not love Him
Are already being punished

By being unable
To recognize
The friends of God

The Most High

He greets the saint
With the peace and blessings of
The Most High

And then asks:

"Where did you come from ?"

The saint says:

"From God"

Taken back by the answer
He asks:

"Where are you going ?"

The saint replys:

"Back to God"

Veto

The world is chaos

I live inside my head

All things are signs in themselves

Every second there are a thousand thoughts
That can be written in several minutes or many months

Today I watched my mother
Suffer in pain
She was immobile

Timing is divine

Before I touch the flower
Its scent touches me

Veto calls

Tells me he's a sinner . . .
Everyone is

Veto keeps it real

He tells me that everyone gives into temptation
It doesn't make you a bad person
Just a weak one

What's scary for many

Is not that they do things that they said they would never do
But that they're actually enjoying doing it

Veto says that
Everything makes you . . . you

We both agree
That those who praise their own outward beauty
At that moment,
Become ugly in our eyes

Outward beauty is common
So don't flatter yourself

Veto ends with this:

Bro,
The world is chaotic,
And that's when you realize that your parents
Are not much different than you
Your parents are just as lost as you are
They too
Are trying to find meaning
In the chaos of this world

Ahmed *(Dedicated to my late friend Ahmed Hussain)*

I had a friend
Who died
He reminded me of God
I met him once in a dream
He hurt me, then hugged me
He still reminds me of God
He died with a broken heart
The world was designed to break your heart
And I feel hollow inside
Friends have become acquaintances
Reflection my companion
I want to start over again with my mother
I know love now
Now I want love to know me

To Him

Where I walk
I walk alone

May the grip of sorrow
Release me from its vice
And let me be on my way

Let my insomnia be for no one
But The One

Let me not use this friendship
For a cheap gain

Let me humble myself before humanity

Let me not dance to my whims
Like dust in the wind
For in the end
We will all be dust

He makes me think of Him
Pray to Him
Write to Him

All for an end
That I may return to Him

My eyes are blank
Without Him

Sleep Walking

Sleep walking
Amongst
Sleep walkers
I am looking for a mirror

I wander in strange lands

They fell in love with who I was
Not who I became

I was lost in a crowd
In a cloud of smoke

Far from the well, to draw water
I am thirsty

The poet and the pen
Are exhausted

Vibe

Guns still stalk
The streets

I wonder where
Their destiny
Will lead them

Ignorance
Breeds
Stupidity

Vibe with me

Lets vibe
Together

This Garden

Our garden
Isn't big
It's a small affair
One in which
We won't lose each other
It's enough for the two of us
The flowers in our garden don't protest in colour
The grass isn't like a carpet
That's soft and smooth to walk on
But for us, it doesn't matter
Because
In our garden
You're the flower, and I'm the bird
I'm the bird, and you're the flower
This garden of ours is small and full of light
A place where we seperate ourselves from the world
And from people

Her Tears

Her tear filled eyes, were locked on his face.
At that moment, hatred boiled within her.
As she said to herslf : why didn't I strangle you,
while you were gently hurting me ?

Awestruck

We were both awestruck
And so we asked ourselves : what is this ?
Love?
Neither of us understood

Hearts Dance

Coming forward into a coloured dance
In front of me, dressed in beautiful silk
Jasmine and roses in your hazel eyes
The fragrance of you is in the air

Writing of loneliness, in prayer, the night arrives
The waters of this soul stir
And in my heart a beautiful song
Pulls all of me into the dance

Live from my life, my door is open for you
So long as your eyes look up at me

As long as my blood continues to flow
Death won't come between us

The Sweet Release Of Death

Almond eyed girl is singing
A sad song in a far away place
A boy is lonely on the harbour, because
Of those who forgot to be happy

Her voice going higher and higher
We who listen, watch the dim moonlight
Kiss and caress her cheek
And her peach dress, like something in a dream

Listen to the padding of her feet on the floor
She is beauty in motion

We're sure happiness will come
Praying for the sweet release of death

Alone

This time
Nobody's looking for love
The drizzle brings down darkness
There's a seagull flapping
With a flick, the day brushes at the gloom
Then swims smoothly
To meet temptations yet to come
Nothings moving
Now the sand and the water are asleep
The waves are gone
That's all
I'm walking
Alone
Drowning the hope
Of getting to the end
And saying goodbye to everything

Haunted Emptiness

I shouted, but no voice answered
My cry died in the frozen air
Emotional numbness
The last dream begged for strength
My heart strangled
Smothering
Freezing
Drowning
Alone . . . I taste ashes and dust
From a left over song
A whiff of that haunted emptiness
Death
And the fever that will stiffen me

Journey

Is this really that long of a journey?
Just a step
Perhaps you can go further
But how?
Why don't you ask the leaves that have fallen
Or ask that quiet chant that becomes a song

What stays behinde to be remembered?
Look at those chickens with their eyes lowered
Or the saddened faces of slaves, or falling stars

How long of a journey?
Perhaps a hundred years . . . Not even . . . Just a wink of the eye
Is something reaching out
Or is something letting go?
Is religion for man
Or is man for religion?
Find your own answers
I'm just trying to kill some time

Caged Dove

Hey you,
Is your job only prayer and praise,
Or is there something that is washed up between them
A dove that, at dawns rising,
Is dead against the bars of its cage?

Back To Him

When I remember how He knows
Every thought
Every breath,
Every heartbeat
I am in awe

When the door is opened
For the caged bird
And it is too scared to come out
That is Him saying:
Come to Me, it is okay

When your world seems dark
More darker than the darkest night
That is Him saying:
I am for you
And you are for Me

When you feel you are far from Him
That is Him telling you
That He is closer to you than you are to yourself
More intimate with you
Than you are with your thoughts

You lay down on the earth
As if the world were flat
And you were nailed down to it

The world is round
So keep running around

For you will run in circles
Back to Him

You look for Him
In temples and shrines
You read your Bibles and Qur'ans
You won't find Him
In buildings and books
Don't look so hard
Rest your eyes
And wait
When the servant is ready
The Master will come

Time Goes On

Time goes on
Where, when and why it's going
I do not know

My eyes glued on
A waiting star

I'm dreaming of a freedom
That's as sure as the stars

I like people who dare to live
People who dare to dream
Those who discover the night
The night that's fragrant with dreams
Rising out of the dust

Time goes on
Where, when and why it's going
I do not know

Remember Me

I speak to You
Out of the suspended silence of the evening
When my chest feels empty
When the clock ticks away

You
Who is woven in secret
Remember me
Let my life live on
Remembering You

We're all corpses
Bless me with meaning
A soldier
Soul journeying for truth
Open my eyes to reality
Close them to illusion

Remember me
The one who lives in these bones covered with dust
There are thousands like me
Lying near the shore

Nabila *(A poem for my aunt. I write, because the page is empty. She is greater than these words)*

Her eyes
Misty and wet
Tell a story

She tells me the words in her heart
Dark clouds follow her
Her life is a gloom
She refuses to let go of the wheel

In living
There is hope

Within this woman
Lives a child
That calls me on days
Where we talk for hours
About nothing

We eat waffles
And tease each other
In those moments
We forget the world
Only to come back to a reality
Too hard to swallow at times

She is a believer

We have a bond
That is inexplainable

Her face is luminous
Giving light to darkness
She gives colour to a world full of black and white
A face
Salted by the sea of tears
Shed,
Everytime she saw the nature of the world

Her eyes are like
Violet stones

She has four lives
She won't desert a single one
A deserter will always be deserted

Fear is taught

Love is natural

I asked her:
"What do you want your four lives to be?"

She said:"I want them to be alive"

O my heart,
In this darkness we are a prayer
That when she reads what this hand writes
Writes out of love for her

She is strength
She is patience
She is love
She is a mother
She is not alone
She
Is reserved for Heaven

I Am

My disbelief
Did not change the reality
Created by the Creator of Creation

I was a lost soul
Soul journeying for truth
I don't know where I stand

I am silence
I am dreamer
I am lost
I am found

I don't know anymore

Understand that this
Is the human condition

I am a prayer
Read me

I am more
Than one person
Know that I contridict
Myself often

Like life

That
Is the point

Lets Fly

Amongst
The green leaves and flowers
The bright open fields
The little innocent children, just old enough to run
Through the fresh rain
To the sound of singing birds and
The sharp, dry wind
The swirling sand and
Lands stripped of everything
We are pressed in babe.
Squeezed and condensed
Sometimes able to take
A single step.
Lets run away
And free our searching souls
To be like doves
Lets fly
Lets learn the ways of the world
Never once meeting or touching
The ground

Wish

Honeyed breezes
Sweet mouthed as a pear

In the twilight hour
With evening falling slow
Almost wiped out like a stain
You declared the birth of a new life

Your shoulder eased me towards dreams
My mouth affirming
What its smile denies

Summer blossoms scent in the air
You were the beginning of a wish
Your eyes take notice of time

Sunsets spent together
My sun shines
To be in your presence again

Some don't believe in God
So why would they believe in me?

Lap Of The Morning

Lying in the lap of the morning
The dawn has just arrived
She tries to find
The heart of her dream
She touches, squeezing
Only the surface of hope
She takes a long deep breath
Along the brink of the valley
Of passion
That has blown away with the wind
Amongst the leaves that become
As gray as dust
The mist of an old, lost love
Is felt shivering for a moment
She stands on the green grass
A breeze rises up
She turns away

Dear Love

Within this sphere
Are those who love to see
All but You

While I
An outer satellite
Dear Love
See only You

Within this sphere
Many choose to look
Under a microscope

While I
Perhaps a rebel
Dear Love
Prefer a telescope

This Ocean

Your love has darkened my star
A moon is rising in my life.

My hand does not
Find comfort in yours.

Your hand is lust.
My hand is love.

Maybe one day
This ocean
Will find its shore.

Mud Skin Boy *(For Tristan Raghunan [Halal Meat] on the loss of his grandmother)*

Mud skin boy
With a little bitta fro . . .

Why you so quiet?

If you miss her that much
Then break your silence

Our whispers do not push at time

There is a hangdrum
Hanging from you

Hit it

Hit it and you
Will hear her heartbeat
Through each vibration

Let it reach
The skin of your ear drum

She is alive in your heart

Look at your hands
The colour of your skin
Will tell you of a rich history

Mud skin boy
With a little bitta fro . . .

You
Are not fire
You
Are burning

You islanders carry a song in your heart

Sing it to me

One Breath

You speak in hush tones
Your breath engulfs me
Absorbed by your fragrance
My anxiety is like lightning

Pilgrimage To Forgiveness

As your senses
Darken

And you feel
No pain

Wake up
In the night

And weep
For your sins

Begin
Your pilgrimage

To
Forgiveness

Amazed

You look at the flower
Amazed by the beauty

I look at the flower
Amazed by the seed

In Thirst

You sit in thirst
Longing for water
The Source
Is closer than you think
Child,
If only
You knew

Silent

Wake up
A new dawn has arrived
And you are still
Asleep

This moment
Is your existence
Yesterdays reality
Exists only in your mind

Do not waste
This moment
Of intimacy with yourself
Sit and be silent
Speeches ruin
Good conversation

Hearts Of Stone

She is emotionally
Checked out from the
Heartbreak Hotel

He stands outside
With a broken heart

Two hearts become frigid

Beats often skipping
Like stones

They know not
What they thought
They once knew

Fighters

Real fighters
Are not violent

Violence is created

When techniques
Cease to exist

These Few Days

Time out for ourselves
Is time for our Friend
The gluttons of society
We will pray for them
For all their hard work
In these few days

Life *[Haiku]*

Long nap,
waking,
life had passed

Smile *[Haiku]*

Smile,
rarely seen,
came twice today

Opened Doors

Sit with all doors opened

Learn how to read the love letters
Sent by the wind and the rain

With the moon appearing
Your mind motionless

The trees
Following their ancient ways

Regret

I don't regret anything
I've done
Because I've learned
From every experience

I regret
What I haven't done yet
Because I have
A lot to learn

This Dark Place

In this dark place
I am a glutton
Typing pieces of this poem
Into my phone
Alone
My thoughts pour out
The pen,
My friend,
Is not with me
My skills
Have abandoned me

By Myself

Your pressence hurts
My feelings

This world
Has a mind of its own

I read poems outside
By myself
The pigeons clap for me

I wonder what life would be like
If I were alone in this world

I'm watching movies
By myslef
In this dark theatre

Feelings

I hate these feelings

Of helplessness
Of emptiness
Of loneliness

I hate
Myself

I kept hearing
It was dark outside

After a while
I began to believe it

I am afraid of myself
I was never afraid of the dark

I don't mind angels

One Day

You were a revelation

I hesitated to
Greet you

Because I knew

We would one day
Have to say goodbye

A Little Bit

I'm a little bit of boy
With a little bit of man

A little bit of anger
With a little bit of laughter

A little bit of fun
With a little bit of boring

A little bit of wisdom
With a little bit of ignorance

A little bit of spiritual
With a little bit of rebel

A little bit of money
With a little bit of broke

Given a little bit of time

To do

A little bit of good

A Single Tear

When I leave this place
I don't want anyone to shed
A single tear for me

I've done a life time of wrong
In a little bit of time

Someone told me
I was their lifes biggest regret

Bullies
Liars
And thieves
Can't hold a light to me

I have tested fatherhood
To the greatest depths

I am a mothers
Worst nightmare

A brother
I am not

I've hurt the ones
That love me the most
I've deceived
I've scammed

I am a hypocrite

Behinde my smile

Is a frown

Behinde my contentment
I am angry

I have been in love
And have the scars to prove it

I'm not even worthy
Of pity

So please
When I leave this place
Don't shed tears for me

I am not worth
A single drop

Poet Poem

Everyone's a poem
Not everyone's a poet

When I meet a poet
I offer a poem

Words

Words do not convey realities
Poems do not contain the spirit of the mind

The ones who attach themselves to words
Are lost

Those who go by poems
Will be sitting in ignorance

Attached

You've attached your heart
To a temporal abode

You are in love
With what loves you not
In return

It will leave you soon
You refuse to believe it

Your claiming to love God
While being attached to the world

Is like

Claiming you're innocent
While holding stolen goods

Some Days

Some days I like seeing your face
Rather than hearing your name

Some days I like hearing your name
Rather than seeing your face

Freedom from both
Will have to do for now

I Remain Silent

Afghan girl says

"If you wanna dance with the devil,
you might as well move"

In the midst of this chaos
I remain silent

One day
I will see death in the face

Overwhelmed,
I will die unto myself

God will be waiting there
When I scream

Foot In The Devils Workshop

I spend a lot of time with silence
Hip hop is laying prone
On the sidewalk
Spoken word is
Trying to revive it

Racism
Still exists

Slavery
Still exists

D.C
Is the last
Legal plantation

Chocolate City

A city predominantly
Black
Working their hides off
For a little
White House
On the hill

Why is Jack Black
White?

Why is Barry White
Black?

Perhaps the same reason
Al Green
Is purple

I'm reeeally bored

This is not me writing poetry
This is me writing foolishness

The Signs

Outside there is
A mystic rain

In my head
A cryptic chatter

The rain pours harder
The chatter becomes louder

Outside
Everything becomes foggy

In my mind
Everything's clouded

And the signs of
Betrayal
Are everywhere

Looking For God Everywhere

An African mothers breasts were cut off
So that her new born baby could not have her milk
She is looking for God
Everywhere

A young Haitian boy
Is eating mud pies on the street
He is looking for God
Everywhere

The alcoholic laying on the street corner
Looks inside his empty bottle
He is looking for God
Everywhere

The young Pakistani girl who was gang raped
Because of false accusations made about her brother
Was looking for God
Everywhere

Amongst the chaos in the world
The gluttons are not satisfied
They are looking for more gods
Everywhere

Two siblings sit in their room
Their hearts beating
Their parents fighting
They are looking for God
Everywhere

An adult male is discriminated against
Because he is a child of divorce
He is looking for God
Everywhere

A young kid is haunted by demons
From his past
He is looking for God
Everywhere

A 25 year old girl is searching for happiness
Without a father figure
She is looking for God
Everywhere

We were all born to die
In between the two
We are looking for God
Everywhere

There were many I would die for
The love was not returned

Betrayed

My heart died a hundred deaths

My worry
Is the pleasure
Of the Most High

A beautiful pattern
Of conduct
I am not

But I see God
Everywhere

No More

He was a victim of her insanity
He told her to take her pretty smile out of his way
And let him go by with his pain
It could be, that he was a thorn to her
Thorns can't hurt flowers
Maybe he made a mistake
Wedding his soul to hers
Even the sun cannot live
Alongside the moon
She came knocking on his door
He said "whatta you want?"
She said "Love"
He said "Love don't live here no more"

Handala

What is it about silence
that causes the soul to sing?
Resonance and wide open spaces
that echo the voices within . . .
One sound following the other,
each note a brother
lyrics and rhythms akin.

In a land not far away,
an olive tree waits.
Branches pointing up,
offering their echos to the heavens.

By an olive tree, a little boy waits.

Memories of a distant past he forgot once existed,
open like flood gates and resonate through his being.
"A man is not defeated when he loses, he is defeated when he
quits"
It's hard to beat something that never gives up.
And so a little boy, hopes, dreams, prays for a better day.

Tomorrows another day.

The world's flattery and hypocricy is a sweet morsel,
and we need to eat less of it.
The way we compel ourselves to "invite people to our way",
before we have even internalized the lessons of that particular way.
Adding toxins to an already polluted environment.

There is a place he touches a silence so complete . . .
this great silence
that comes in the moment after the wind dies.

By an olive tree, a little boy waits.

Bodies raped and pillaged.
Decapitated and mutilated.
The ugliness of this world,
they will soon leave behind.

A genocide in Palestine . . .
an open air prison.
Ethnic cleansing at its worst.
Humans caged like animals.

The smell of rotting flesh is in the air.

And a check point is to the point,
depending on their mood.
Soldiers getting full authority,
with infantile education.

Little children screaming "Allah!"

Death and change,
the two constances in the world.

By an olive tree, a little boy waits.

He wants to fill what's empty and empty what's full.

He doesn't want to be among those people engaging in
futile discussions. With no depth, no substance to them.
Preoccupied with their own dreams and emersed in their own
fantasies.

A deep love, for the ephemiral beauty of a fleeting world.

And people don't understand the reality of the world,
until they are tested with a loss . . .
and then they come back to God.
Cause the world gives and then takes back.
It builds for you, then ruins it.
People are too comfortable to care.
And even if they do care,
they carry the burden of caring.

A moment of silence, won't bring a life back.

So this little boy,
wants to follow the ones who can see,
not the ones that are blind.

By an olive tree, a little boy waits.

Zionists hijacked Judaism,
created a new golden calf in Israel,
exploited the Holocaust to justify Israel's existance,
and adopted their terror techniques directly from the Nazi's.

And so,
by an olive tree, a little boy waits.

Sick of bandwagon REVOLUTIONISTS.

Diseased hearts impregnated the world,
evil is what it bore.
They're not pro peace,
they're just anti-war.

Telling those afflicted to get it together
and pull up their boots.

Yeah, very well put.

Failing to realize,
that the oppressed have been waiting for a while now,
standing bare foot.

And the truth will never change,
only your perception of it.

You feeling social? You feeling just?

By an olive tree, a little boy waits.

And where he walks, bitter steps follow.
But in his struggle, he finds his hope.

Anything that has a beginning, has an end.

And so he prays,
to wake up to a sunrise.
To watch the sun splash colour onto the world before his eyes.

He wants to colour the world beautiful.
So that his people are no longer occupied, subjegated and op-
pressed.
So that life is no longer cheaper than a barrel of oil.

So,
by an olive tree, a little boy waits.

And for his people, the price was too high.
So they payed in blood, to avoid the goodbye.

And the truth is the most powerful ally,
so he can wait, without getting tired of waiting.

For every star has its sky.

Dawn is just breaking, and the incense is burning.

And by an olive tree, a little boy waits.

And Palestine is the David in this epic event,
of Biblical proportions.
And peace remains a distant hope.

And we've upped our standards,
so UP YOURS!

War is the unfolding of miscalculations.
And old soldiers never die,
just the young ones.

By and olive tree, a little boy waits.

He wants to be taken back to a place
in time where he hasn't been.

Turn your ear to the volume of real life.

Because a story . . .
makes up the majority . . .
of history.

And ignorance is not bliss . . .
So it's time to get right . . . or get left.

The truth hurts,
but lies can kill.

By an olive tree, a little boy waits.

As he oversee's the world's largest concentration camp,
he knows that the truth is on the side of the oppressed.

Children with stones in their hands,
will re-invent the world.
And they will remain precious in his heart.

This land will never die.
It always revives.
This land will always strive.
Those hills will always grow,
olive tree's, pure honey and natural cheese.
This land is not used to strange concrete,
and seperation walls.

And Handala waits.

And we wait.

People with hearts of gold and intellects of mercury . . .
to see Handala turn around and finally smile . . .

A smile on his face,
his scars and tattered clothes replaced with something greater.

But until then . . .

By an olive tree, a little boy waits.

Love Poem

My heart left . . .
and so did she.
I don't know whether I should go after her
or after my heart.
So I asked myself,
"self" . . . "what do I do?"
Self said: "Go in search of her,
because you need a heart
in order to find her.
If she's not there,
then what would you do with your heart?"

Distant shadows are moving closer.
Every path I choose,I will see its results.

I made her cry.
So many nights, she wished
that she could drown me in a pool of her tears.

I always showed my face, but never my heart.
She is a voice to my heart.
Her words,
are like sweet melodies that penetrate souls.

And just like that,
she was forgotten.
Like a passing love, and a rose in the night . . .
she was forgotten.
And as I stood outside and looked at the sky,
with its kohl darkness,

I had never felt so alone.

"Life is beautiful with you",
I wanted to tell her.

I remember when I first saw her . . .
She was alone,
and I was in front of her beauty alone.

The hours are never the same.
Each minute is a memory.
And what will I write after her to another lover . . .
if I ever love another?

I used to see her in my dreams often,
and she gave it meaning.
She was healthy and happy.
Smiling.
Her smile made my soul want to fly away.
Eyelashes long.
Lips red like pomegranates.
She was full of life.

I don't see her anymore.
Haven't in a while.
But I pray she's alive and well.
Or maybe she died,because death loves suddenly, like me.
And death, like me, doesn't love waiting.
But for her, I will.
Waiting for hope,
waiting for a lover who,
perhaps,
might not arrive.
Maybe this longing is my way of surviving.
Lovers, the likes of us don't die,
not even once,

from being in love.

She said: "What will we do with love? Should we take it with us
or leave it behind?"
I said: "Let it go wherever it wants. It has already grown."

I pray a moon will rise from my darkness.
And I pray for her,
the salaam of Heaven and Earth.
My soul looks upon my body through her fingers.
We were extensions, of each others soul.

We were two strangers from two far away lands a while ago,
yet
how much of me is you?
Tell me I'm necessary for you, like sleep.
There is no limit to me with you.
I was given your love to subsist on.
And if you ever come back, you'll find what you left here,
waiting for you.
My heart was too heavy for my body,
so I let it go.
Tie a rope around my heart.
Hold on tight.
Don't let go.
Take my hand,
let us laugh the night away.
There was a love that passed through us,
without us noticing,
and neither it knew nor did we.
We will soon return to our tomorrow, behind us,
where we were young in love's beginning.

Our time wasn't enough to grow old together.
Memories of a shy beginning,
put a smile on my face.

Innocence and admiration known,
but not said.
So we let love be unknown,
and the unknown a kind of love.

I am who saw his tomorrow when he saw you.
In the hazel of your eyes, I feel small.
You are loves' confession.
Got me love-sick.
I like you a whole much of a lot.
You are priceless, and worth nothing.
You remind me of what the world feels like.
And I will be in your history forever.

No one knows what I keep behind my eyes.
She looks at me, like she's looking at me for the first time,
and says: "You want me to feel regret? There are no tears left
in my eyes."

But she's inseparable from my heart.
My eyelids never close,except that she is between them and my
eyes.
To me she is a rose.
A woman who loves my deep brown eyes.
She is a jelly bean.
Hard on the outside,
soft on the inside.

Like seeds dreaming under the snow,
my heart dreams of Spring.
Take me back to the water,
before the storm.
Leave nothing out,
tell me the whole story.

I ride misery through the night,

love sewn in my chest.
Stumbling through the dark,
I failed to see your light.
Now your fire burns me.
May our flames dance again someday.

I'm trying to find answers for questions,
and questions for answers.
Not all those who wander, are lost.
We are those wanderers.

I struggle for sleep
but am denied
by the screams
in my ears,
as they beg,
and yearn,
for your gentle voice again.
They remember a smile in your voice.
"There is no greater sorrow than to recall, in misery, the time
when we were happy"
The world 'aint all sunshine and rainbows . . .
the mystical realization of our existence.
She was the melody of a weather storming in my heart.
We were luminous silhouettes in moonlight.
She is a rare pearl filled in the inside with many jewels.
She remains precious in my heart.
And there is no other reason, but reason itself.
I was willing to destroy myself,
if it meant bringing her closer to me.
You know this song,
so I don't have to sing it for you.

I could write you forever.

You are as beautiful as a bird-filled summer.

My tongue is fragranced with the mention of your name.
Memories of a distant past,
immersing me with emotions . . .
of a time I once used to love.
What more can I say, that hasn't already been said,
or isn't already known.

Meet me at the crossroads,
so I can have someone to walk with.
"Loneliness is the most terrible poverty"
Often I feel a whirlwind of emotions . . .
the kind you get when moms and dads fight.
Like those who live in beautiful houses,
but have broken homes.

My heart waited for an eternity to be touched.
I sent kisses to the wind,
hoping the wind would touch your face.
Will we remember
what we forgot
we already knew?

We will fill the book of our life
with brilliant pages.
Whether we are together or not,
you will always have a piece of my heart.

And this kind of love makes you never feel alone,
because we'll always have each other.
The kind of love you can't predict,
a spontaneous combustion of our hearts.

A time will come . . .
A moment when,
a light will shine through the dark,
when you will no longer have to fill in the blanks,

when we will be free of the worries of the world,
the moment we learn to love ourselves,
the moment you're ready to share your world.
At that moment . . .
I will come for you.

Why

I'm 23 years old and I'm sitting in a mosque.
Doing my daily litany's
Conversing to God
Thumbing a rosery

A man enters the room,
And in doing so,
Takes away the silence
And holds
My attention

He begins to speak:
"Brothers and sisters
There is a young boy
Muhammad
9 years old
Visiting us from Saudi Arabia
He has bone cancer and
He is having one of his legs amputated
He is here alone
If any of you, has any time
Please
Do go
And visit, this young brother"

I find myself sitting in a fixed position
The thought of this young boy
Occupies my mind

I don't know why I feel like

I need to see him
But I do

I long to see this stranger
Who knows me
Just as well as I know him

However
I find that we have 3 things in common

He shares the name of my Prophet
He is Muslim
And we both occupy space
In this little place
Called Earth

So I go

But as I go
I become hesitant

What if he's miserable?
Cause I'm sick of miserble people
Trying to make everyone around them miserable

And the shard of doubt
Turned in my head
Piercing within it
Second Guesses
But I try to fight those things that
Put me in the same category as those
Who have a distorted perception of reality
Of humanity

I open the hospital door and
Fixate my eyes on a

Frail
Dark skinned
Almond eyed boy

Sitting in his bed

He looks at me and smiles
I smile back
I couldn't find the right moment to break into the silence
So he does it for me

"Asalaam alaikum assalam wa rahmatullahi wa barakatu"
May the peace, mercy and blessing of God, forever more be yours

My name is Muhammad

"Wa alaikum assalam wa rahmatullahi wa barakatu"
May the peace, mercy and blessings of God forever more be
yours as well

I'm Ja'far

I sat on the bed and began to talk to him
He
However
Was lost
Lost in a world that until now
He had only heard about

For in me
He saw a world
The he only understood
Through a box of colours and images

As I try to hold onto my last bit of reality
As I try not to pass over the world of insanity

I ask myself:
"Is this how it's supposed to be
Having to lose all those
Close to me?"

I find it hard to accept that
This little boy will have his leg taken away from him
In days

I find it hard to accept that
This young boy
Only has months
To live
I find it even harder to just sit there
And listen to him
For his every word
Seems to cling to the beat of my heart

Life has yet to free me
From the madness that it continues to unfold
And these days
I hate being alone
Cause when I'm alone I think too much
And I don't look through the eyes of amazement
But I look through the eyes of reflection

And on many a level
Everyday our flesh and bones
Have to deal with the Devil

And as I sit cross legged
In front of this little boy
Who refuses to touch his plate of rice and chicken
Until I
Take the first bite

"Sahtain"
He says to me

"May you be given double the reward of this meal"

I ask him if he's scared

He says:
"No condition is permanent"

His lips smile
His eyes are sad
And as I look into his eyes
His eyes shine wet

I comfort him

We joked and talked
I offered him a chocolate bar
And he finds it to be a special occasion
So he allows himself to indulge

He wants to be seen
Without being seen

As I left the hospital that night
I lost my smile
For I couldn't face the nightmare
I knew would come

For I loved him
But I never told him

He was soft spoken
But hard to forget

I wanted to
At that moment
Carry to him
Hymns of
Who he was

And though he was hidden from my sight
He was not absent from my heart

I tell my father
Of this little boy
Muhammad

About our conversation
About how he
Always wanted to watch an American movie
About how brave he was
About how he was
Wise beyond his years

I told my father
How I was scared for him

And he told me to:
"Leave it in the Hand of the One in Whose Hand every soul is"
And that if I didn't have full conviction in Allah
Then he as a father
Had failed to teach me anything

One too many midnights later
I wake up to pray for the well being of this little boy
Praying for a miracle
Praying for him to stay with us a little bit longer

I walk through the halls of my heart
My screams never loud enough to be heard

I open the hospital door

There
He sits

His leg covered with a blanket
He looks at me with no smile
He extends his hand to shake mine

I hold it
Light as a feather
For he is weak
Almost lifeless
From the chemo

The cancer has spread throughout his body
No ones told him
But he knows

He tells me that I'm the only one that understands him
And so he trusts me

He says to me:
"I know I'm gonna die
I've accepted, that I'm going to die
I just wish that people would stop acting different around me
Always trying to cheer me up and be really nice to me
Asking me if I want to hear a story

They tell me everything
Except
That I'm going to die
Why don't they just tell me that I'm going to die?"

I thought I would die when I heard that
And as I cried on the inside

I mustered up everything I had
To contain myself

And all I could say to him was

"Why would you want to hear something . . .
That you already know?"

Let Us *(For my nephew Arman)*

Let us indulge with grandma and grandpa,
but be balanced with mommy and daddy.
Cause daddy's are for fun, and mommy's
mean business.
Let us hold hands and laugh the night away.
Let us speak the truth.
Let us smile.
Let us remain pure and innocent.
Like angels . . . let us be light.
Let us be the light when it is dark.
Let us get excited to hold new born babies.
Let us be those, who make people want to be good again.
Let us have popsicles and ice cream on a cone that melts.
Let us make ice cream soup.
Let us be tickled so that we may laugh uncontrollably
with our eyes closed.
Let us make sand castles and snow forts.
Let us make snow balls and snow men.
Let us . . . be those snow angels.
Let us be the tears of joy in people's eyes.
Let them melt in us, like chocolate in the sun.
Let us swing on swings and slide down slides.
Let us climb monkey bars, until like astronauts, we can touch
the sky.
Let us fly kites and run in the park.
Through fields, let the willows chase us.
Let us have no worries in the world.
Let us jump rope and hop scotch.
Let us play dress up.
Let us have a lollipop for every baby tooth we loose,
for we will loose them all anyways.
Let us have plump, rosey,

squishy wishy mooshy wooshy cheeks.
Like little apples.
Let us be the apple of your eye.
Let us be full of life.
Let us run in the rain and
roll down hills.
Let us be read to.
Let us imagine, to be whatever we want to be.
Let us be dreamers.
Let us be curious.
Let us ask questions.
Let us collect rocks and sea shells.
Let us have grass stains on our knees,
and scrapes on our elbows.
Let us look out the window and day dream,
observe the actions of others.
Let is be full of love . . . showered with hugs and kisses.
Let us pray to God.
Let us stay up late at night, and whisper to each other.
Let us pretend to be grown ups.
Driving cars, and chasing bad guys.
Sip tea from cups with our pinky's up.
Let us make lemonade with lemons.
Let us see the good in the bad.
Let us see beauty in ugliness.
Let us not mock any creation of God,
for He makes nothing less than perfect.
Let us scribble out of the lines in colouring books.
Let us think outside of the box.
Let us wish for more wishes.
Let us play and then fight.
Let us play fight.
Let us fight and make up.
Let us play hide and seek.
Let us secretly take sips of coffee.
Let us cry until we can cry no more,

and fall asleep.
Let us be mesmorized by stars and fire crackers.
Let us be thrown up, so we can fall into waiting hands.
Let us get a new toy everytime we go shopping.
Let us watch cartoons and sing songs.
Let us trade lunches.
Let us be free from duality.
Let us have chocolate milk with twisty straws.
Let us stay awake all night, before the first day of school.
Let us open doors,
and free caged birds.
Let us run around all day . . . burn out,
then take naps and drool on our pillows.
Let us override cries with laughter.
Let us remind people how to be kids again.
Let us brush our teeth and gargle . . . Play with daddy"s shaving
cream.
Let us have food fights and draw on dolls.
Let us jump on beds and wrestle with pillows.
Let us pee in swimming pools.
Let us have popcorn and waffles,
cereal and gum balls.
Let us scream loudly . . . then be silenced . . .
then scream again, cause we forgot.
Let us go on car rides, and fall asleep
in the back seat.
Have mommy and daddy take us to our room.
Tuck us in.
Let us sleep.
Let us dream.
Let us,
be children.

Misery Loves Company

It's funny how the world comes to me
as I realize that misery loves company
And I wish for once, that I could put on her shoe
So I could understand
What I had put her through

And I wish I could go back in time
Again and again
Until in her
I'd find my childhood best friend

So that no matter how much we'd yell, scream and fight
We'd always make up, and things would be alright
Cuz we'd fight over things that never really mattered
And meaningless fights would only leave us shattered

A time where
The urge to rebel would obsess my mind
A time where Bazooka bubble gum and red,white and blue
popsicles
We would seek to find

And I would finish mine and wait for her
Cause she would always take long
And she'd give me hers, and I'd refuse
But she would insist
Nevertheless

And as I'd take it
I'd say, "don't love me so much, that I may die out of happiness"

And if real eyes
Could realize
Real lies . . .
Then I swear by the One in Who's Hand my life is
That her eyes
Could extract the poison out of my lies

And when it comes to me
She's the only one that can say
"No one knows him, like I know him"
She's the ink in my pen, occupying my thoughts . . .
My
Living poem

So as I release these words
From the prison of my heart
To the gates of my mind

These words that were once confined
Can now find
A place to rest in someone's heart . . .
In someone's thoughts . . .

As it flows into them from me

It's funny how the world comes to me
As I realize
Misery
Loves company

Increase Tha Peace

In an effort to increase the peace,
I'll read this piece
For your consumption
And my release

Because I refuse to stop writing until
I can reach even one
Cuz they say that the night is darkest
Just before the dawn

And so I refuse
Like Allah refused to raise the sun
Until Bilal gave the adhaan

And my words, like Islam
Are enshrouded in peace

And Islam was a movement
Cause the move meant that
Men, women and children would not accept defeat
And it caused a nation to stand on its feet

And colours didn't matter
As long as they worked as an entity.
Cause as Muslims
We are empowered by our diversity
And there is no justification
For gentrification
Human stagnation
Human rights violation

Female genitalia mutilation
Coersion, apparatus, capitalistic oppression
The cause of a people's great depression
And being born a Muslim
Doesn't make you the product of a violation

You don't see anything wrong with
Piercing a child's chest with bullets
Or bulldozing houses with sleeping infants?
Holding back a mother by her hair
Telling the father to calm her?

If it weren't for the power of Islam
To give meaning and sanity
To the lives of people

Then everyone in Palestine
Would be a suicide bomber

So I sat my 2 year old niece on my lap
And asked her where is Allah's house?

And she was so innocent and pure right from the start
She said, "Allah's house is in your heart"

And so I realized
That to know Him,
I had to go through His prophet

Cause when he came to Medina
He eliminated all the plague and disease
And then from this world he would depart

Now
If he could eliminate all the plague and diseases from a city
Then imagine what he could do for you

If he lived in your heart

And though the devil hides in detail
The chains of Shaytaan
Weren't made so strong

And it was a matter of time
Until my birth
That I too
Was born into this caged illusion
Of air, moisture and earth
And for what it's worth

I want be able to say to everyone that I
Love you
And that if you draw a small circle and exclude me
I will draw a bigger circle
And include you

Realizing
That you are my brother in faith or my equal in humanity

And it's insanity
This world that we live in
But I try to keep it together
Cause I'm too old
To lose control

And there are times when I want be left alone to meditate
So I can prolong my spiritual state

And control my sins
And baptize the jinns

And I'm sick of some girls
Degrading their worth

Running around half naked
With not enough consciousness to say

"Wait"

"This is a mistake"

And
"I need to get out of this state"

Cause the devils trying to seal her fate

And I'm sick of reality TV
And beauty pageants

And every other sick institution
Of glorified prostitution

So I say
Reflect people reflect

On all that you were
And all that you want to be

And all those you saw
And those you can't see

And your forte
Should be the lyrical foreplay

Cause expression
Is the natural cure
For oppression

And a fuel ignited in my soul

Inside this bottle of tales

Ready to explode like a
molotov cocktail

And I will aspire
Until I expire
Cause I was taught that
Words were meant to speak the truth

And that you should evaluate your tongue
Before you've begun
Cause it's hard to apologize
Once the damage has been done

And I was brought up to respect women

And though many resist
I still persist
Cause I still believe that
Chivalry exists

So I want to teach the mind
And reach the blind

And though I'm a class clown
In a class of my own
I still have a strong perception

And sometimes temptation
Is thrown in my direction

And sometimes I feel oppressed

And as a poet
Sometimes I find myself obsessed

With things like
Love, music and revolution
And dreams of finding a solution

A solution for the spilled blood in the holy land
Crying out to God

A cry for peace

A solution to end war
Bloodshed and tears
And weapons of mass destruction
Are between George Bush's ears

And the problem isn't with Islam or Judaism
The cause of the occupation is only Zionism

And you can't kill innocent people
And expect to go to heaven

And terrorism didn't begin
On 9/11

Giving less taxations
To partnering associations

And as much as the media filters things
They wanna run and hide

History will still tell you that
America was founded on genocide

And death to the Apartheid

And I pray for a world
Full of love

Where things are just and fair

But I may not be here
If we ever get there

But I stay positive
Cause it's never too late

And a smile is a curve
That sets everything straight

The world turns away from us
Faster than we can turn away from
It

A lot of laws
But very little justice

Internal wreckage of the soul

Scatter and tatter
Lost in the gray matter

Justice delayed
Is justice
Denied

But His delays
Are not
His denials

So learn to think for yourself

It's knowledge with understanding
That you want to acquire
And ignite a fire

That makes you wanna inspire

And don't jut take my words
Cause I don't preach to no choir

Let me decide how the truth will affect me
Don't make that decision for me

And the one who has intelligence
Subdues himself

And I wish I could sink my teeth
Into the core of everyone's pain

Turn around and plant a love sonnet
In the warm summer rain

And the poets make the language make sense
Of everything around them

So I say to you

Let's observe the world
Like we've never seen before

Through the eyes of
A child
A newborn soul

Violence was never the remedy

So make peace

And pray

For your enemy

I Love Her *(Dedicated to my special lady)*

I love her like
Peanut butter loves jelly

But I'm not talking about food
Cause only a glutton finds sweetness
In the belly

Her beauty leaves me breathless
As she radiates magnificence

It's a shame many don't know That

Pride is ignorance
And ignorance is bliss
And they know this

And that's why they take pride in not knowing
We're not growing
And I'm just aimlessly flowing
Until I see her
And on my sleeve
My
Heart starts showing

And when I feel chills
And I begin stu stu stu stutter
She
Wraps her arms around me
And gives me
The lovers cover

And if they were to stab me a million times
I would only bleed more reasons to love her

I looked her in her eyes, and said

"How can u love me so much
And expect me to believe that it's true?"

She said,

"This life that I live isn't for me
It's for you
And He gave me gray skies
So that yours could be blue."

And though she makes me so mad at times
Makes me wanna curse

But I hold back
And I don't wanna ruin this verse

Cause in my yester years
She quenched my thirst

They say

"Forget her and everyone else
Just follow us
Aim high and make all your goals lateral."

But I had nothing without her
So I put my soul up as collateral

Shouldn't surprise you
Cause that's what lies do

And when my soul had turned into a bird
That found the right spot for its nest

That's the day I realized
That she would be my hearts strongest weakness

Because she carried me
Where no one carries anyone

And she fed me from the fruit of her heart
That which no one feeds anyone

And she will live forever
Incomparable

Because beauty and infinity
Are inseparable

And if I were to die
And be buried under the earth

I would rise on the 23rd hour
Just to prove to her
That I couldn't live a day without her

Held so close in life and love
As destiny takes control

She gave me a body
To encapsulate my soul

This poem is about her
And no other

The one responsible for my physical being

My mother

Lover's Quarrel

It's been a while since I've done this
Emotions being born from this manufactured world

Sweet love
Has left a bitter taste in my mouth

Reason and love lived bare in my heart

Now my heart has split through all the joy
And no one wants to retrieve this lost heart

It's been left behinde

Behinde in a dark place

There
The shadow lives and does not travel with me

Time will always show us the final flower of the day

And no matter what
The brightness of our love will remain alive

I refuse to regret what I've been given from you

For it was you
Who taught me the mystical ways of love

It was your poetry that made me believe
That love still exists

Through you
I knew what it felt like to be loved

It was your light that lit this dark soul

The thought of not having you around
Hit me with a surge of emotions

Like an immense wave
Crushed me
Againt a hard stone

So I ask you to
Tie your heart to mine

And together

Let's you and I

Seal the silence

Knocking On Her Door

Feeling lost
Confused
Irritable
At a cross roads

Helpless and misunderstood
Frustration seeping through
This scarred soul

Haunted
By the misleading images
Shown to me

Screaming from the inside

Spoken word
Words not heard
And is it absurd

That these days
Sunshine and breezes
Reflecting and smiling
These things make me happy?

Paradoxal
Trying to find pleasure
Some sort of attachment to any good that's left in this place
While trying to detach myself from it.

And I don't think I'm the only one that makes that resolution

To escape this delusion
A victim of the worlds illusion

And I made a promise to myself
That I would never do what I did

If all He did
Was give me another chance

And I lied to myself
As I came back for another dance

And now

Now I stand here
A victim of my own oppression
And I'm pressin' hard,
Tryina break though

Set free

But as much as I try

I'm left here empty inside

Alone

Alone with my thoughts

And all I think of
Is her

Her smile
Her depth
Her warmth

The smell of her breeze
That brushes my face
When she walks by

Those eyes,
O those beautiful eyes
Smile at me even in my dreams

And I wish

For even a moment
To be transported back to that day
That place
That very moment
That had made the boy wanna be a man

Where time had ceased
And my heart had opened

And I walked through that door
To knock on hers

And as she opened that door
She smiled

And let this stranger in

A visit so brief
But so sweet

I promise to come back
With a love much deeper

And as I look at her
In full blown beauty

My heart and words exhaling out
Everything that I take in from her

Everything I see
Everything I feel

I inhale all of her
Back into me

Until we meet again
I'll hold my breath

Until I come knocking
On her door again

The Soma

You won't know how I feel
And all the things I've gone through
Behinde this smiling mask
I'm too hood to be true

Eyes well up with tears
And the soul just cries
Nowhere to go to
No girls nor guys
Startin' to get tired of these minor
Spiritual highs

Hypocracy is evident
No matter how many tries
Cause these real eyes
Realize
Real lies

So I drank the soma
And the world dissappeared for a while
Then He sent you to me
And made my eyes smile

A blessing you are
But I'm still empty inside
Cause I went to the world
And from Him I'd hide

Should've seperated the love for Him and the world
Right from the start

Cause the love for Him
And the love for the world
Can't sit
In a single heart

Lovers Cover

Don't speak of your suffering
When God is speaking to you

Many claim to love God
But the real lovers are but a few

None like suffering
Though they desire the cause of suffering

Veiling not only their eyes
But their hearts with a covering

So tear down the veils
And then you'll understand
The answers are waiting
To be taken by the hand

Inspiration descends down
Like blessed pearls from above

Binding your eyes, heart and life
Into a thing called
LOVE

Un-Invited

I look out at the dark sky
waiting for the sun to embrace this beautiful day

My heart beats slowly
to my souls dismay

Battling my nafs
Trying to contain this desire

The desire is not of this world
But for something much Higher.

My emptiness I cannot speak of
It's something that I feel

The remedy for this
Is closeness to The Real

He gave me this feeling
Filling it to the brim
How can I complain
When this longing is from Him?

He does this to me often
That I may turn and come back

When I start to stray away
And faith is what I lack

Now the birds start chirping

And quickly fly by

Taking in what they can
Of the cold gray sky

I lay here hungry and cold
Trying to fill this void

When close to Him
I'm filled and overjoyed

So I lay here waiting
For I will not fight it

Love and death both come
Un-Invited

Don't Be Afraid

Just as the reed bed cries
Of seperation from the flute
So too, does my soul cry
For union with the Beloved

People chase after the shadow
And forget about the Real

Why take the shell
When you can have the pearl?

Don't be afraid,
Dive deep into the Ocean
Dive deep, and forever be drenched
With the sweetness of Love

The rock that is touched by rain
Shall always be a rock

So be ye, like the earth
Which softens with each blessed drop

How foolish I am
Trying to explain Love with words

Silence
I shall speak no more
What you need to know about Love
Lays in your hearts core.

After So Long Love Has Come

After so long
Love has come

After so long
I am awake

Such a Love this is
Not even sleep could overtake

Where shall you go
Once I depart?

O my friend, not to my grave
But to those who knew me
For I shall live in their heart

I am so small
Yet this great love exists within me
I have come to speak of Love
For Love shall set us free

I speak of Love
So that you may learn

We all come from Love

And unto Love
We shall return

So lose your SELF

That you may cleanse your heart

The Lover shall come
When YOU depart

Is This Love

Surely, for every beauty
He has created an eye to see it
I too have been blessed with an eye
To see the face of my love
The evanescence of her beauty
Makes me not want to sleep the night
For so long
I dreamt of the moment
When we would finally meet
Words and time cease to exist
When I think of her
Now she's appeared
My dreams
Become a reality
She looked at me and smiled
I remained silent for a little while
And then smiled at her
She smiled back . . .
Our conversation was over

Me And You

There's a fire in my heart
That burns for you

There are moments in the day
When I think of you

There are breezes that blow by
And I feel touched by you

There is a scent in the flower
That reminds me of you

There are days of seperation
That makes me long for you

There are days you yell at me
But I can't get mad at you

There are moments of silence
And all I want is to hear from you

There are days when you're late
But I still wait for you

There are days when you worry
And I pray for you

There are days when you're goofy
And I smile at you

There are days when I'm down
And I wanna be held by you

There are days when I'm hungry
And I wanna be fed by you

There are days when I'm stressed
And I want comfort from you

There are days when I have nothing
But I wanna give to you

There are days that I'm bad
And I need patience from you

There are days I hate shopping
But not with you

There are days you drive me nuts
But I still want you

There is no day that goes by
Where I don't think of you

Everyday I thank God
That He has given me you

The Land Of The Stolen Poets
(Written By Wafa Auochiche and Jafar Alam)

"What should we do with them?
Burn
Incarcerate
Incinerate
Murder or mutilate them?"

The options were plenty but the assembly opted for exile.
Some members even suggested Nazi torture techniques
Of course, Guantanamo Bay was a convenient option
Another sanction
But in the end
Exile was the final solution

And so they took them one morning
One early morning

There were hundreds of them
Hundreds of us

Because I was also part of this strange mélange

We were hurried and told the boat departed at 5 o'clock sharp

5 o'clock sharp
Sharp like the tongues of the exiled
Sharp like the tongues of the poets and the deported ones
Spent countless days and countless nights on the ship
My mind sailed and wondered
What would heal my mother's pain
And what would appease my father's sorrow
Perhaps a poisoned arrow in their hearts would ease their ache

I spoke to the ocean and asked him to sing me a song
About all the African slaves it engulfed
But he remained silent
And so did the deported ones

I know what silence means

Silence is shame
And embarrassment at times

I know the ocean is too ashamed to divulgate such numbers

And so we sailed and arrived to the land of the stolen poets

Upon the arrival we were told that our only crime was poetry

Some cried at the irony
Others attempted to slice their veins vertically
And the rest laughed hysterically

I just stood by and read the inscriptions on the large banner

"Welcome to the land of the stolen poets
You are convicted of two crimes against humanity

1. Poetry
2. You have messed with the status quo

You are no revolutionary
You are a criminal
And shall remain here until further notice
You're now sentenced to burning books of poetry, until they
cease to exist"

And so we burnt them
We ripped and burnt them

Asking a poet to burn Rumi, Gibran and Victor Hugo's words
Was like asking the women of pre-Islamic Arabia
To bury their newborn female infants alive

And so we burnt their words from morning to night
Exhausted and too tired to put up a fight
We obeyed and complied

From time to time around midnight
We would all gather around the fire
And share little poems that we didn't have the courage to burn

Some rolled tobacco around Gibran's words and inhaled them
'til the morning light

Welcome to the land of the stolen poets, where possession of
pencils, pens and ink are criminal offences which often result in
severe sentences,
Welcome to the land of the stolen poets, isolated and starved
like the West Bank and the Gaza Strip

We spend our days inhaling the essence and fumes of poetry,
making love to metaphors
Similes and personifications became our only temptation, passion
and only act of fornication

But the plan back fired
Burning page after page
Intoxicating people
Like the smoke of sage

And the poetic floetry flowed
As the poet's flow
Gave birth to a new poem
For every seed that it sowed
Intoxicating each one with the soma of a dead poet's prose

Each word breathing life into the empty crevices of lost souls

Uprising

Verbal intercourse
What the poets crave
Offering freedom like an emancipated
Berber slave
And mother Earth
Gave birth
To poetry
Holding poets in their infancy

Singing

"Hush little baby don't you cry
For I'd feed you the truth
Before I ever fed you a lie
And the words of the righteous live on
Even after they die"

(whispers: Let us free the poets and ourselves)

"SILENCE!! How dare you speak what you feel!?
How dare you stand for something!?
Don't you know?
I will take your words
And in the ocean I will throw it
For you are in the land
Of the stolen poets"

We ate guavas peaches and metaphors for sustenance
And kept the similes for the rainy days
And had rhymes as delicacies

We whispered poetry to butterflies and birds
Hoping the migrating ones would spread their wings and the
words

We had silent poetry slams
Turned them into sacred annual jams

Until one day it all came to a halt

For poetry ran course through our veins
We bled poetry
Exiled from the rest of the world

We were rounded up
Shackled
Tongues and fingers mutilated
And dipped into the bitter sea

Bitter sea
Adding to the wounds
Insult to injury
Humiliated and demoralized
Nonetheless poetry still remained our luxury

See what they never understood
Is that the fumes from the books we burnt on a daily basis
Reached the nostrils of the folks who knew nothing of our crisis
And all they felt was a poetic aroma engulfing the whole of humanity

And slowly, but surely, they all turned to poetry
They breathed and dreamed its essence

Much like us
When we gathered around the fire
And allowed it to penetrate our souls

And one day
We took up arms
Mau Mau style

We learnt from the Maroons and the runaway slaves of Jamaica
and Cuba

We followed the pattern of the Haitian revolution

1804 sir !

I said

1804 sir !

You know we had to mention it's the first country in the
Caribbean
That freed itself from the white chains of slavery

Anyway

So we took up arms and taught them a sweet lesson
Bitter sweet for some
But all we intended to do
Was revive the spirit of a nation gone numb
Numb (heartbeats)

Can you hear it?

Its begun

The bloodless revolution has begun
Mission failed !

I said

Mission failed !

For what they had failed to realize
Was that they
Were now living

In the land
Of the endless
Poets

Your Love

Your love is like a cloud
That passes the sun kissed sky
Unable to differentiate a breeze from the wind
As time floats by.

Love tore through the veils
In my heart it did reach
For this kind of love
No imam could even preach

Guide me now
For I have lost my way
Do not deny me Your love
For this I do pray

What use do I have
With worldly things?
I've been pierced now
With Love's beautiful stings

Along with the wind
Do take me away
To that Eternal garden
Where the angels do pray
To that place, where everyone's
Free like the dove
To that place
Where every moment there is only Love

I make sujood, for I love You

More and more

O Allah

I pray that You would lower the floor

So I may humble myself
To the King of king's
Like the Shakoor
I don't care what this life brings

This life will end
And then everyone will see
The Truth was You
It was never we

Who are we, but a creation of Thee?
Break these chains
And set me free

They'll wrap me in shrouds
And lower me in the ground
I was once lost
But now I am found

Now I'll leave, to go and pray
Pray that today, would be that day
The day they'll lay me
And over me they'll pray

Pray that I would reach such a place
Where everything is beautiful and full of grace
I couldn't ask for anything better
because You and I, would be together

Once Upon A Time

Once upon a time . . .
I used to carry a beautiful song
In my heart

Once upon a time . . .
I used to have
Colourful dreams

Once upon a time . . .

Still not old

So why do I feel
Ancient?

Hey

Hey

Lets stop majoring
In minor things

Lets escape ourselves
In each other

And sing an eternal love song
To beauty

Lets tease
The ears

And if you're not up to lovin'
Don't do it

But if you are
Then come

Hey

If it doesn't work out

We can always
Breakup

Feel Me

I
Just feel

And my pen
Just bleeds

Those who understand this

Sometimes
Cry

You feel me ?

You Are The Moon

Let your mind
Bubble up
In the sunshine of
Optimism

Honour
Love's coming

You are the moon
My love

We are not people
Of war

Lets learn together

Teach me
To
Teach you

Learn Love

You wanted to know
Where you could learn
Love

Go to the same place
Where you can learn
Life

You will find it

Between tears

Heartbeats

And

Aching spirits

Betrayal

Everything good to you
Isn't good for you

You were the seamstress
That tailor fitted
My pain

Anything in a bad persons hands
Can be a weapon

And betrayal

Takes on many forms

Brudda Safi

Brudda Safi says to
"Value your values
And
Secure your securities"

We've been serving
Too many masters

"Watch me now"

When your life starts to count
They will respect you

So pursue a higher quality of life
Even if you have to start the journey
By yourself

Child
You have to walk the road
To actually
Meet it

For God
Will not do anything for you
Unless

You are willing to participate
In your life

Your Smile Called

Your dimples resemble
The crescent moon

Under which we've danced
So many nights

Learn to be a child again
Maryam

To fall
And get back up

Your smile called

She said she's jealous

That means she misses you

We already dove into the ocean
Of each others soul

And dreamt dreams
That jumped

In the sky

Afghana
(For Almond Eyes)

In the voice of the night

I stand
In a pool of light
From under
A street lamp

I'm not looking for
Something

I'm looking for
Everything

I'm a member
Of my
Remembering

I remember everything
That I don't want
To forget

The sun begins to rise
In a drunken stumble

Afghana calls

Like a reunion
With a friend
Long thought
To be dead

Passing lifetimes

Through our mouths

This day
The sun is endless

And my heart
Is full

Brown Boy Blush

Everything about you
Is bright

You are sunshine

You know poetry
Like your heartbeat

You know love
Like your breath

You know God
Like a breeze against your body

O Lawd

Almond Eyes

You bout to make a

Brown
Boy
Blush

Human Nature

Driving home

In this gray
Drizzly morning

"Human Nature"
Is playing

I imagine myself
Driving to you Maro

Thoughts of life
Leaving me

Before one last meeting
With each other

In human form

Obsess my mind

Birds fly
Black
Against the sky

Rain droplets
Freckled across
My windshield

Parked

In a plaza lot

Mike
Fades out

My Favouritest Person
(For Almond Eyes)

You are

The most evolved human being
I know

You are worth
Kept promises and endless arms

You deserve to never stop smiling

Worrrrd

I feel like we've exchanged so many words
Without having said anything at all

You are a refreshing beauty

Aw shucks . . .

You're my favouritest person

In the world

I Miss

Almond eyes

I'm an old soul
That still believes in
An indescribable love

You saved my heart
And my smile

I asked you:
"What do you miss?"

You said:
"I miss love"

Me too

You said:
"I miss laughing til my stomach hurts"

"I miss running after the ice cream truck"

"I miss picking dandelions"

"I miss . . . innocence"

Maryam
Your voice is
A dove and moonshine

Almond Eyes Hears The Dove's Cries

Let me swallow
The sky

Hold tight to your dreams

Take in the sun
And shine

Maro Jaan
(For Almond Eyes)

You sit
With bubu jaan and maadar
And think of me

I think of you

And ask

"What are you doing?"

You reply:

"As I live in love
So I shall die in love
As there is nothing else
Left to do"

Praise be to God

The Light of the World

Just quoted

Nur Jahaan

Long Lost Friend
(Dedicated to Almond Eyes)

You are miraculous
In your strength

Remember to keep your smile
Sacred

You are like the full moon
In your beauty

Radiant
As the sun

Keep lovin'
And you'll find it

Don't feed your pain
Let it starve

Everyone's gettin' at you

There are stories and secrets
Written on your face

Your smile
Is a shortcut

To my heart

Going through broken times
You were a lesson learned

Jafar Alam

A breeze
Learning to dance at night

You know lonely

Like a long lost friend

Its Own Reward
(For Almond Eyes)

Let my downfall be
That I love you

When you can't
Love yourself

I have a deep love
For Afghans

Because in them
I see you

I see hope

I see pain

I see struggle

You inspire me
More than you know

We cannot measure
How much the heart
Can hold

The toughest lessons I've learned
Had to do with love

He the Most High
Is with me

I go out alone

But I am not
Alone

Love itself
Is its own reward

The First Dream Ever Dreamed

The night arrives

With the gentle
Whispering kiss
Of a thousand snowflakes

We have spoken our prayers
Filling the wind with it

Could I put my heart into you
And get yours in return?

Let the moon reflect the words
I could not find

I'm everywhere
And you are never there

We are emotional creatures

Standing in hunger

My ribs and muscles
Stand from my skin

I live in possibility
Look me in the eyes
And I just might love you

Sweet sweet dawn
Let me get a taste

Answer
As the first dream
Ever dreamed

Times Gone By

The afternoon gives up
The summer sun

The anxious evening says goodbye
To the dying day

Colours dance and die
Across the sky

They raised their glasses
Full and high

And drank to toasts
To the times gone by

Peace of Mind

Choose the path of self-knowledge
Over accumulation of facts

And the path of self-expression
Over image enhancement

And reach your destiny
With a peaceful mind

That will give you
Peace of mind

And Then She Said Goodbye

Lust was a sweet thing you caught
And held with the eye

She was yours for a moment
And then she said:

"Goodbye"

Jafar Alam

Free Functioning Mind

Let your mind become
Agile and free

Like a mirror

That grasps nothing
And refuses nothing

My Symphony

Beauty
Is the music of this soul
Made visible

And you

Are my symphony

To Know You

To know you
I do not need to empty my cup
Entirely

I just need to prepare some room

To meet the complete
You

For Haiti

Dear Thursday,
How we gonna do this?
A broken truth results in a broken heart

Dear Self,
The world goes on with and without you
Within and without you

Words are words
And actions are actions

You
Are magic made

Dear Haiti,
It's about that water
I'm all about bringing you this water
Hold tight babe, we gotchu

I speak of YOU as ME
Of I as US

When did we remove ourselves from each other?

If I shine, we all gon shine

The revolution starts with love

Dear Love,
Hold me like a revolution

And who says you can't be a revolution all unto yourself?

Dear World,
Wake the hell up

It serves us nothing to argue with each other
About why tragic events occur

What matters
Is what we do to respond to these matters

Lets vibe for a minute, shall we?

Things serve their own purpose
It's not our job to argue purpose

It's our job to live
To live abundantly and with humility for each other
Yes?

Maybe this is a sign
A sign that we are too isolated from each other
Maybe ...
Maybe they were all signs

The test of our character is what we'll do
Once we've seen the cheekbones of suffering
After we've seen the sweat of its brow

Remove the debris and rubble so you can be free
And when you get free, reach back and help someone else

The pendulum of the mind alternates

It's much easier to keep track of the truth

No right mind
Would wrong you

Turn the page
And write a new chapter

I squint to read what is written
On the faces of these ungrateful days

Deep in your heart is a mind

Our life
As it nears us
Is an inescapable reflection of how we look at it

Tomorrow holds
Tomorrow holds all
Tomorrow holds all that is possible

Haitians
They have stories

They have stories
But no one that will listen

They have secrets

They have secrets
But no companion to keep it

Show me a scar
And I will kiss its face

And just cause they're breathing,
Don't mean they're living

Freedom 'aint for free

Let's die to the past every moment

The confusion
Confuses me

Every tongue will have to confess

The conversations getting lonesome

The depth of certain thoughts, untouched by words

An ocean of formless feelings

I understood the word of the wind and the trees

A child
Is crying on the street

Her tears could be my own

Walking on blood stained soil
Their smiles collapsed

And don't speak to me of LOVE
If you don't know BROKEN

And don't pretend to care about something
Just cause everyone else seems to be about it at the moment

You thought it was a joke?

HELL to the NO

The earth is talking back
And she's letting us know the deal

We stand side by side
But we don't even see the same thing

Some days, ask questions
Some days answer

Let inspiration be your drug of choice

Lost in a storm of broken dreams

People ugly from ignorance
And broken from being poor

The earth, rich and pure
Clinging to bodies

We are losing love every hour

People have a right
As human beings
To live

That is our birth right
Not our privilege

And some are in the business of making money

But we
We are in the business of making magic
That's what we do

A little child asks me:
"Where does love come from, and where does it go when it's
gone?"

I said:
"Child, you have beautiful words that make my heart cry out
for you"

Greed makes
Breast filled revolutions go shirtless

I was hoping they'd bring me flowers
From the last grave they buried their minds

My grandma, she told me:
"In the heart of men, there is a boy weeping for love"

I believe in miracles

In Haiti
The sun shines on darkness

The caged wall sings

They're fixing sidewalks
But hardly any feet to walk on them

Little Haitian boy, eating a mud pie with your sister
If no one told you they loved you today
I love you
I love to love you
Know that you are brilliantly beautiful
You are my melody

I am an offering
Make of me what you will

And know that change requires death
But also produces life

Change is constant
And
God is change

And in case there is a heartbroken individual that comes across
my words
There is a new risen consciousness born from the rubble of
pain

Rest a while
My child
There will be angels in the morning

And somewhere in Haiti, there is a severe wound miraculously
healing
Somewhere in Haiti, a child is dreaming of a family, of a full
stomach, of a hug
Somewhere in Haiti, there is a woman breastfeeding an orphan
And somewhere a grandfather is singing a prayer to calm his
people before rest
And somewhere there is a child still surviving under the
rubble, being saved

There are angels everywhere

And we have not stopped praying

And I want to want to
Pray for cold hearts to be warmed
For the impossible to make believers out of non believers
To pray for a miracle

Write your name on every pain
Sadness hunts murdered dreams

Love …
Love is a friend left in exile

O faces of beauty
Give your features some meaning

You sit under night's lantern

Sad for your sadness

The streets are empty
Like death

And what do I know
About the pain of death?

I don't even know
About the pain of birth

And I swear by The Living God
That we are losing the race against time

And where did they magically find
These American soldiers in Haiti?

I'm just saying, that
If they treated American citizens like refugees
In New Orleans
Then how do you think they'll treat Haitians?

I guess they sent soldiers to save face and to
Politely control a nation through its suffering

And it's not really the soldiers
It's the people that sent them
Soldiers are meant to carry out orders
No matter how good

America's greed, doesn't just end at oil
It never even began there

It was always about land and power

And all you have to do is consider any great leader
That doesn't support the agenda of American colonization
And you'll understand the depth of this system

Soldiers are bred to kill or be killed
They're not bred to empathize and heal
And they felt good, because they sent soldiers to Haiti?

You don't send soldiers to a country to heal people
Weakened by hunger and deprivation

And don't call it a conspiracy theory
Just because you're too afraid of the world you live in

Some things are just real

Some things
are just REAL

Speak to the force within you
That which is trying to escape and set free
Let it fly

Let us have a
World-driven vision

You already know what it is

We are greatness bound
It was written

A victim offers me a cup of her salty tears

I used to know these three chicks:
Shoulda, Coulda and Woulda
And boyyy did they love to waste time

In my head
I hear their screams sound like multiple stabs in my ear

Her people are prisoners
Their words taken away

They are cell mates and soul mates

But in the silence

Who
Will speak for them?

Dear Thursday
Dear Self
Dear Haiti
Dear Love
Dear World

Thanks for listening

PEACE

For Now

Your eyes for now
Are puffy and red

Your longing for love
For now

Is dead

An Old Friend

Almond eyes

Reading my poems
You are not so much
Reading a book

As you are visiting
An old friend

Persevere Maryam

There is a world awaiting your kind

You are a magnificent breed of
Future generational love

The children will demand more

And your strength
Far outweighs any person
I've met

My Story . . .

You speak of your pain
Through your tears

But who will listen
To my story?

"... I cry on silence's shoulder til it drowns in my tears ..."
-Maryam Noori